T0319066

Cambridge Elements ≡

Elements in Perception
edited by
James T. Enns
The University of British Columbia

Special Editor for Attention
Marvin Chun
Yale College

ATTENTIONAL SELECTION

Top-Down, Bottom-Up and History-Based Biases

Jan Theeuwes
Vrije Universiteit Amsterdam
Institute Brain and Behavior Amsterdam (iBBA)

Michel Failing
Charité – Universitätsmedizin Berlin

CAMBRIDGE
UNIVERSITY PRESS

University Printing House, Cambridge CB2 8BS, United Kingdom

One Liberty Plaza, 20th Floor, New York, NY 10006, USA

477 Williamstown Road, Port Melbourne, VIC 3207, Australia

314–321, 3rd Floor, Plot 3, Splendor Forum, Jasola District Centre,
New Delhi – 110025, India

79 Anson Road, #06–04/06, Singapore 079906

Cambridge University Press is part of the University of Cambridge.

It furthers the University's mission by disseminating knowledge in the pursuit of education, learning, and research at the highest international levels of excellence.

www.cambridge.org
Information on this title: www.cambridge.org/9781108813068
DOI: 10.1017/9781108891288

First published 2020

A catalogue record for this publication is available from the British Library.

ISBN 978-1-108-81306-8 Paperback
ISSN 2515-0502 (online)
ISSN 2515-0499 (print)

Attentional Selection

Top-Down, Bottom-Up and History-Based Biases

Elements in Perception

DOI: 10.1017/ 9781108891288
First published online: August 2020

Jan Theeuwes
Vrije Universiteit Amsterdam
Institute Brain and Behavior Amsterdam (iBBA)

Michel Failing
Charité – Universitätsmedizin Berlin

Author for correspondence: Jan Theeuwes, J.Theeuwes@vu.nl

Abstract: In this Element, a framework is proposed in which it is assumed that visual selection is the result of the interaction between top-down, bottom-up and selection-history factors. This Element discusses top-down attentional engagement and suppression and bottom-up selection by abrupt onsets and static singletons, as well as lingering biases due to selection history entailing priming, reward and statistical learning. We present an integrated framework in which biased competition among these three factors drives attention in a winner-take-all fashion. We speculate which brain areas are likely to be involved and how signals representing these three factors feed into the priority map that ultimately determines selection.

Keywords: top-down and bottom-up control, attention, selection history

ISBNs: 9781108813068 (PB), 9781108891288 (OC)
ISSNs: 2515-0502 (online), 2515-0499 (print)

Contents

1 Introduction

In everyday life, we constantly look around and use our visual input to guide our behavior. We may search for our favorite coffee in the supermarket, attend to the soccer ball when the striker tries to score a penalty kick, or search for the specific color of our child's sweater when picking her up at the daycare. Typically, we try to focus our attention on relevant information and ignore information that could distract us. The act of paying attention, focusing on only objects and events that are relevant to us, can be considered to be under volitional control. Just as we can decide to pick up a pencil, we can decide to pay attention to the teacher in front of the class or to the messages coming in on our phone. Yet this volitional act can sometimes be disrupted by a salient and/or unexpected event that calls for attention even when we had no intention to look for it. For example, we may inadvertently attend to the road worker wearing a fluorescent orange safety jacket, a flashing item on a website or a waving hand in a crowd.

Because the visual world consists of many more objects than we can process at a given point in time, we need to focus our limited resources on relevant information and filter out distracting information at any moment. Selective attention is the mechanism that determines what we see and act upon. Attentional selection has been considered to be the result of the interaction between intentions or goals of the observer (current selection goals) and the physical properties of the visual environment (salience of the objects). For example, when driving down the road the goal may be to attend to all objects that are relevant for the driving task such as road signs, crossing pedestrians and traffic lights that may soon turn to red. At the same time, attention may be captured against the driver's intentions by a moving billboard along the road-side, or a telephone flashing on the dashboard.

It is generally assumed that the interaction between these two different types of processes determines the priority by which information is selected from the environment. Basically all prominent models of attentional control have described attentional selection as the result of this dichotomy sometimes referred to as bottom-up versus top-down processes (Corbetta & Shulman, 2002; Itti & Koch, 2001; Theeuwes, 2010; Van der Stigchel et al., 2009a), stimulus-driven versus goal-driven selection (Egeth & Yantis, 1997; Ludwig & Gilchrist, 2002), exogenous versus endogenous attention (Carrasco, 2011; Posner, 1978, 1980; Theeuwes, 1994a) or automatic versus nonautomatic control (Jonides, 1981; Shiffrin & Schneider, 1977).

Given this dichotomy in attentional processes, over the past twenty-five years or so, scholars have held a considerable debate whether "pure" bottom-up, stimulus-driven, exogenous attention (i.e., selection against one's intentions) exists. According to one prominent view, pure bottom-up attention does not exist as attention is always the result of top-down intentions (Folk, Remington & Johnston, 1992). On the other hand, proponents of the existence of pure bottom-up attention have claimed that events that are salient enough will be selected irrespective of the top-down setting even when they counteract the current goals (Theeuwes, 1991a, 1992, 1994b, 1995, 2004, 2010; Van der Stigchel et al., 2009a). When that occurs, one speaks of *attentional capture*, signifying a condition in which objects or events receive processing priority independent of the volitional goals of the observer (Theeuwes, 1992). When such an object or event not only captures attention but also triggers a saccade to the location of the event, this is referred to as *oculomotor capture* (Theeuwes, Kramer, Hahn & Irwin, 1998; Theeuwes, Kramer, Hahn, Irwin & Zelinsky, 1999).

Even though the discussion regarding the extent to which processes are controlled in a top-down or bottom-up way has been very instrumental for developing attentional theories, a recent review of Awh, Belopolsky and Theeuwes (2012) pointed out that this classic theoretical dichotomy may be ill defined and no longer holds as attentional selection is in many cases neither the result of current selection goals nor the consequence of the physical salience of objects. Awh and colleagues (2012) suggested a third category, which they named "selection history" to stress that the history of attentional deployments can elicit lingering and enduring selection biases, unrelated to top-down goals or the physical salience of items (see also Theeuwes, 2018, 2019).

The role of top-down, bottom-up and history-driven effects in attentional selection is illustrated by Figure 1 (adapted from Theeuwes, 2018). All signals project onto an integrated priority map believed to represent a comprehensive framework accounting for selection priority. The priority map is considered to be a winner-take-all neural mechanism guiding the allocation of attention (e.g., Fecteau & Munoz, 2006; Itti & Koch, 2001). It is assumed that the three factors determine selection weights within the spatial priority map at any moment in time. Within the map, these weights are combined into a single topographic representation of the environment that determines the selection priority (e.g., which location is selected first, second, third, etc.). Individual signals acting on the priority map originate from sensory input (bottom-up), current goal states (top-down, or behavioral relevance) and selection history. At any given time, these priority signals compete with one another. For example, the attentional capture effect discussed earlier demonstrates that bottom-up salience signals may be so strong that they, at least initially, overshadow goal-driven selection (Theeuwes, 1991a, 1992, 2004, 2010).

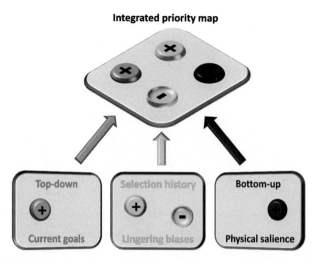

Figure 1 A schematic representation of a priority map that integrates three sources of selection bias: the observer's current selection goals, selection history and the physical salience of the items compete for attention (adapted from Theeuwes, 2018).

According to this new framework (Awh et al., 2012; Theeuwes, 2018), the role of selection history in attentional selection is much more prominent than previously assumed, and it is important to reconsider the role of top-down and bottom-up selection. We argue that many studies that have claimed to investigate top-down attentional control were actually investigating history-driven selection. In the following sections, we thus define in more detail what is meant by top-down, bottom-up and selection history–driven selection and how these selection modes may interact.

2 Top-Down Selection

It is not immediately clear how to exactly define top-down attention selection and definitions are typically broader than those of bottom-up attention selection. Yet one aspect that is often either explicitly or implicitly included is the notion of "volition" or "act of will," typically involving some conscious, intentional act of selecting a particular object. In other words, the selection is considered to be under the control of the observer (Theeuwes, 2018). Just as I can decide to type in a particular key on my keyboard, I can decide to direct my attention to the upper left side of my computer screen. After processing the information at the top left side of my computer screen, I may decide to direct my attention to the cup on my desk and take a sip of coffee. In essence, at any point in time, the observer is deliberately in charge of what to select. Many definitions stress the aspect of volition. For example: "a slower, top-down mechanism with variable selection criteria, which directs the 'spotlight of attention' under cognitive, volitional control" (Itti & Koch, 2000, p. 1490); "the former [endogenous attention] is a voluntary system that corresponds to our ability to willfully monitor information at a given location" (Carrasco, 2011, p. 1488); "volitional shifts of attention are thought to depend on 'top-down' signals derived from knowledge about the current task (e.g., finding your lost keys)" (Buschman & Miller, 2007, p. 1860); "attention can also be voluntarily directed to objects of current importance to the observer" (Connor, Egeth & Yantis, 2004, p. R850); "voluntary orienting can be considered aspects of top-down attentional control"(Hopfinger, Buonocore & Mangun, 2000, p. 284); "top-down visual attention is a voluntary process in which a particular location, feature, or object relevant to current behavioral goals is selected internally and focused upon" (Katsuki & Constantinidis, 2014, p. 515); and "volitional top-down process, which can exert its influence through acts of will"(Baluch & Itti, 2011, p. 210).

Even though many agree that top-down selection should include some aspect of volitional control, not everyone shares this view (see Theeuwes, 2018). Sometimes top-down control is defined as anything that is not bottom-up or stimulus-driven – that is, any type of attentional selection that cannot be considered to be externally controlled. Some authors use "broad" categories such as anything that is not perceptual (Egeth, 2018) or any type of selection that is influenced by "context, learning, or expectation" (Gaspelin & Luck, 2018c). Some downplay the volitional aspect of the definition of top-down control by arguing that top-down control can occur without deliberate intent (Sisk, Remington & Jiang, 2018) and that top-down control can be involuntary without awareness (Gaspelin & Luck, 2018c). Even though, in principle, there is nothing wrong with using these broad labels of top-down control, one should realize that with broad definitions it becomes impossible to pinpoint effects based on the moment-to-moment top-down intentions of the observer and those based on the selection history (Wolfe, 2018). It is thus conceptually important to understand that attentional control through intentional volition is completely different than control that is the result of previous experiences (Awh et al., 2012; Theeuwes, 2018).

2.1 Top-Down Attentional Enhancement

Because of these arguments, we use the stricter definition of top-down control and imply conditions in which attention is completely under the control of the observer. In other words, top-down selection is completely volitional: at any time, a person can choose at will from the environment what to select. One classic example that it is possible to direct attention "at will" is a study by Posner, Nissen and Ogden (1978). In this study, a centrally presented symbolic cue (e.g., an arrow) was shown to the observers before display onset. This cue pointed to the location of the upcoming target with 80 percent validity. In other words, in 80 percent of trials a centrally presented arrow pointed to the location where the target appeared. In 20 percent of the trials the target appeared at the "invalid" location (i.e., at the location opposite to that indicated by the arrow). The results showed that observers were faster and more accurate when the target appeared at the cued location than when it occurred at an uncued location. Typically, relative to a neutral condition in which no information about the location of the upcoming target is given, there are performance benefits and costs. These types of studies are typically interpreted as evidence that observers can direct their attention (not their eyes) covertly to the location indicated by the cue. As a metaphor, directing visual attention to a location in space has been compared to directing a mental "spotlight" that "selects" parts of the visual world around us (e.g., Posner, 1980). The key point of these experiments is that the location to which observers are required to direct their attention varies from trial to trial, indicating that the focus of attention can be truly shifted "at will" from one trial to the next.

Similar to Posner and colleagues (1978), Theeuwes (1989) also investigated top-down orienting by means of a centrally presented arrow. This study compared the efficiency of location cueing (pointing to the location of the upcoming target) with that of shape cueing (presenting the shape of the upcoming target, a diamond or a circle). The reasoning was that if shape cueing is just as effective as location cueing, one expects that any information (regardless of whether it is the location or the shape of the target) should result in performance costs and benefits. In other words, one expects cueing on the basis of shape to generate the same effects as location cueing. Observers made a speeded discrimination response to the orientation of a line segment positioned in either a circle or a diamond shape presented either to the left or right of fixation (see Figure 2). Consistent with a spotlight model of attention, the results showed clear reaction time (RT) costs and benefits for location cueing (see Figure 2), but not for shape cueing.

It has been argued that shifting of attention in response to a centrally presented arrow (as was originally done by Posner, 1980) is not necessarily top down as an arrow pointing to a location in space has properties that evoke automatic orienting to the location indicated by the arrow (e.g., Ristic & Kingstone, 2006). Even though this may hold for arrows, several studies have used other means to direct attention to a location in space. For example, Vecera and Rizzo (2004) used the words "right" or "left" to direct attention. Theeuwes and Van der Burg (2007) employed measures derived from signal detection

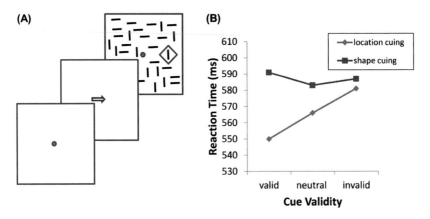

Figure 2 Stimuli and data from Theeuwes (1989). (A) With a validity of
80 percent, the centrally presented arrow indicated the location of the upcoming
target. Observers responded to the orientation (horizontal or vertical) of the line
segment presented within a target diamond or circle shape. (B) Reaction time
(RT) for cue valid, neutral and invalid conditions. For location cueing (blue
line), relative to the neutral condition, there were clear RT costs and benefits.
Cueing the shape of the upcoming target (whether it would be either a circle or
a square) had no effect on RT.

theory to investigate the efficiency of location cueing. They used a truly
endogenous location cue in which the likely target position was indicated by
a number corresponding to the hour indication of an analog clock (e.g., 12 is the
top location, 2 is the top right location, etc.). Also, unlike earlier studies that
have used relatively short stimulus-onset asynchronies (SOAs) (typically
300–600 ms), Theeuwes and Van der Burg used an SOA of more than one
and a half seconds so that observers could prepare optimally for the upcoming
target. The results indicated that top-down shifting of spatial attention was very
effective (detection sensitivity A' = 0.90 for valid versus A' = 0.75 for invalidly
cued location), demonstrating that even a relatively abstract and cognitively
complex cue results in strong location cueing effects. Crucial for this discussion
is that the location of the target (one out of twelve locations) varied from trial to
trial and observers were perfectly able to use location information from arbi-
trary cues to shift their focus of attention to the target prior to its onset. This
suggests the deployment of true volitional top-down attentional control.

2.2 Top-Down Attentional Suppression

Just as it is possible to actively enhance the processing of information presented
at a cued location in a top-down way, one should be able to actively suppress

a location where distracting information is likely to appear. Even though this assumption appears to follow almost naturally, the evidence for active top-down suppression is mixed. One of the first studies to address this question quantitatively used eye movements as the dependent measure (Van der Stigchel & Theeuwes, 2006). In this study, observers were informed if and where a distractor would be presented. A central cue was presented that consisted of a short arrow pointing toward the location of a possible distractor (80 percent probability) and a long arrow pointing toward the target location. When the target appeared, observers had to make a speeded eye movement toward the target location. The idea was that by means of top-down expectancy observers should be able to actively inhibit the location of the upcoming distractor. The results showed that by pre-cueing the location of the distractor, the eye movements toward the target were affected, as the eyes deviated away from the distractor location even when the distractor was absent. Because eye movement trajectories that curve away from a location have been attributed to the inhibition of that location (Sheliga, Riggio & Rizzolatti, 1994; Theeuwes, Olivers & Chizk, 2005; Tipper, Howard & Jackson, 1997), these results provide evidence that observers actively inhibited the distractor location on the basis of a cue indicating its location, even in trials in which the distractor did not appear.

Ruff and Driver (2006) conducted an fMRI experiment in which observers performed a speeded discrimination task wherein a centrally presented arrow pointed to the location of the upcoming target. The color of the arrow was either red or green, informing observers whether a distractor would be present or absent on the upcoming trial. If a distractor was present, it appeared always on the opposite side of where the target was presented. In control blocks, the target arrow did not provide information about whether a distractor would appear. The results showed that observers were generally slower when a distractor was present relative to when it was absent. However, in those trials in which the upcoming distractor was cued, reaction times were faster compared to trials in which this information was not available. Critically, when the cue indicated that a distractor would be absent, reaction times were similar to those found in the control blocks in which no distractors were presented. The conclusion was that advance knowledge of an upcoming distractor helps to counteract its impact, thereby resulting in faster responses to the target. The fMRI data showed that when a distractor was validly cued, activation in the corresponding hemisphere (which was never the hemisphere corresponding to the processing of the target) was higher, suggesting that an active process was taking place at the cued distractor location. In other words, these results seem to indicate that cueing the location of the upcoming distractor resulted in active inhibition of this location, allowing faster target detection.

In another study, Munneke, Van der Stigchel and Theeuwes (2008) explicitly cued the location to be ignored as the target was never presented at that location. Observers had to search for a target (a capital "B" or "F") that could appear in one of four fixed locations on the screen. On some trials, a cue was presented pointing to one of the four locations, indicating that the target would not appear in that location on the upcoming trial. That is, the cue always only indicated the location at which the target would never appear. The results showed faster responses following cue trials compared to neutral trials in which no location was cued. In addition, either a lowercase "b" or "f" was present as a nontarget element on all trials. On cued trials, this lowercase letter appeared in the cued (to-be-ignored) location. The idea was that by creating a compatibility effect similar to that observed in the Eriksen flanker task (Eriksen & Eriksen, 1974; see also Theeuwes & Burger, 1998), it would be possible to measure the attentional suppression of the to-be-ignored location. The results showed less interference from these lowercase letters in cued trials than in neutral trials, suggesting that the letter at the to-be-ignored location was actively suppressed. Others have reported similar findings showing that cueing observers to ignore or inhibit nontarget locations can speed up search (e.g., Chao, 2010; Serences, Yantis, Culberson & Awh, 2004).

In contrast, Moher and Egeth (2012) investigated whether it is possible to inhibit a particular distractor feature (e.g., inhibit the color red). The results indicated that simply inhibiting everything that is red in the display is impossible. It was shown that the location containing the feature that ought to be inhibited (e.g., red) needed to be first spatially attended before inhibition could be applied. In other words, actively suppressing the color red by using a pre-cue was not possible. Interestingly, they showed that observers were only able to ignore the feature when a premask containing the to-be-ignored feature was presented for at least 800 ms before display onset, suggesting that it takes time to first attend to and then inhibit the location. Even though the goal of their research was to demonstrate feature suppression (e.g., suppression of the color red), Moher and Egeth (2012) showed that pure feature suppression may not exist but instead that it can only occur after the location containing the feature has been spatially attended. They dubbed the strategy of first selecting to-be-ignored items at a location in space and then suppressing them the "search and destroy" mechanism.

Yet another account that assumes that distracting information can be suppressed in a top-down way is the "signal suppression" hypothesis of Gaspelin and Luck (2017, 2018b; Sawaki & Luck, 2010). This hypothesis is particularly concerned with how stimuli that generate a strong bottom-up signal can be suppressed. Gaspelin and Luck (2017, 2018b) employed the so-called additional singleton task originally developed by Theeuwes (1991a, 1992) to study distractor suppression. In this task, observers search for one specific and clearly defined salient singleton (e.g., a diamond among many circles) while another singleton irrelevant for the task (e.g., a red shape among many green shapes) is simultaneously present. The typical finding is that the irrelevant distractor singleton interferes with search for the target singleton. However, when a different search mode is adopted (i.e., the feature search mode), it is assumed that observers can impose top-down selectivity, which should eliminate capture by salient, irrelevant stimuli that do not match the attentional set (e.g., Bacon & Egeth, 1994; Leber & Egeth, 2006). In other words, by applying top-down control, it should be possible to prevent capture by the irrelevant salient singleton (Bacon & Egeth, 1994). Consistent with this idea, Gaspelin and Luck (2018a) showed that when observers adopted the feature search mode, the salient distractor no longer interfered. Critically, they also showed that when this distractor was presented in a lateralized location, the distractor positivity component – a component referred to as the P_D component and shown to reflect suppression (e.g., Burra & Kerzel, 2014; Eimer & Kiss, 2008; Hickey, Di Lollo & McDonald, 2009; Sawaki, Geng & Luck, 2012; Sawaki & Luck, 2010) – was found in the ERP signal. Notably, however, some studies have failed to find a P_D component (see Barras & Kerzel, 2016). However, one aspect that seems critical for suppression to occur in these circumstances is set or display size. More specifically, studies that have found a P_D component used an unusually small display size (typically only about four elements in the display) while studies that did not report a P_D used large display sizes (more than four elements). One possible explanation is that when small display sizes are used, none of the singletons (neither target nor distractor) stand out from the background, allowing for suppression to occur (see also Wang & Theeuwes, in press).

Other evidence of distractor suppression comes from behavioral studies employing a so-called dot-probe task originally pioneered by Kim and Cave (1995). Gaspelin, Leonard and Luck (2015) showed that observers were less likely to report a probe presented in the location of the salient distractor than at all other locations, suggesting that this location was suppressed. Specifically, this finding was interpreted as evidence that the location of the salient distractor is suppressed below baseline. In another study, Gaspelin and Luck (2018a) combined these findings and showed that the magnitude of the lateralized P_D component correlated with suppression as observed in the probe task.

Even though active top-down suppression may be possible, the evidence is not always convincing, particularly when the information that needs to be suppressed is highly salient. In Wang and Theeuwes (2018a), a central cue pointed to the location that needed to be suppressed. At this location on some trials, a highly salient distractor singleton was presented. The results indicated that this type of trial-by-trial cueing (i.e., cueing the distractor location) was not effective in reducing the interference effect caused by the distractor. However, presenting the distractor during a block of trials much more often in one location than in all other locations *was* effective in reducing the interference effect. This finding is similar to what was reported by Noonan and colleagues (2016), who used a variant of the Posner cueing task. Here, observers were centrally cued to either the location of the target or the location of the distractor, or no predictive information was given. They found the classic Posner benefits for cues indicating the target location both in blocked (the location remained the same during a whole block) and in mixed (cueing on a trial-by-trial basis) conditions. However, distractor cueing was only effective in the blocked condition and could not be achieved on the basis of trial-by-trial cueing (similar to Wang & Theeuwes, 2018a). Noonan and colleagues (2016) concluded that flexible top-down mechanisms of cognitive control can only be applied to target facilitation. Distractor suppression, however, only emerges when predictive information can be derived directly from experience.

In addition, a recent study provided direct evidence that suppression in an active way is only possible when there are no salient elements in the display (Wang & Theeuwes, in press). In Wang and Theeuwes (in press), the letter-probe task of Gaspelin and colleagues (2015) was used while participants engaged in feature search. It was found that suppression below baseline as reported by Gaspelin and colleagues could only be observed when four search items are on display. For larger display sizes (i.e., 6 and 10) that Gaspelin and colleagues did not use, and when both the target and distractor singletons were salient enough, they found no evidence for suppression. Instead, and consistent with a stimulus-driven account, there was clear evidence that the salient distractor captured attention. Wang and Theeuwes (2020) argued that signal suppression as advocated by Gaspelin and colleagues can only occur in displays with a limited number of non-salient elements.

In summary, the evidence for active top-down suppression is less clear-cut than evidence for active top-down enhancement. Top-down suppression seems possible under conditions in which the information that needs to be suppressed is not very salient (e.g., Munneke et al., 2008). However, it appears that in order to apply suppression, one needs to first spatially attend the location, akin to what Moher and Egeth (2012) called the "search and destroy" strategy. In general, most evidence suggests that, if anything, suppression is spatial in origin even though others have argued that suppression can also be feature-based (e.g., Gaspelin & Luck, 2018c). An alternative possibility is that instead of suppressing one cued location, observers may have enhanced the processing of information at all other locations. Such a mechanism would imply that what has been interpreted as top-down attentional suppression is, in fact, still top-down enhancement.

3 Bottom-Up Selection

Pure bottom-up attentional control lies outside the organism and is completely driven by the properties of the environment. In its most extreme form, it is assumed that as soon as a specific stimulus appears, attention is immediately directed to that stimulus. In his seminal work, Posner (1980) labeled it "exogenous attention" and referred to this attentional capture response as a physiological reflex. Later, Neumann (1984) referred to bottom-up attention as an automatic process and stated that "automatic processes are under the control of stimulation rather than under the control of the intentions (strategies, expectancies, plans) of the person" (Neumann, 1984, p. 258). Stimuli that are salient – that is, stimuli that stand out from their environment – are assumed to grab attention in a bottom-up way. Numerous computational models have stressed the role of salience in attentional selection (e.g., Itti & Koch, 2001; Itti, Koch & Niebur, 1998). These models basically take an image as input and process it in parallel across various feature channels using different spatial scales. The end result is a set of topographic feature maps combined into a saliency map (Koch & Ullman, 1985).

3.1 Bottom-Up Selection by Abrupt Onsets

It is generally agreed that suddenly appearing new objects, or so-called abrupt onsets, are very salient and have the ability to capture attention in a truly bottom-up way. The finding that abrupt onsets capture attention dates back to the early research of Eriksen and Hoffman (1972) and Jonides (1981), which showed that observers' attention was automatically drawn to a cue presented with an abrupt luminance onset. Using saccadic eye movements as their dependent measure, Todd and Van Gelder (1979) revealed that stimuli presented with an onset were detected faster than the very same stimuli when presented without an onset. Yantis and Jonides (1984), by having observers search for a specific target letter embedded in an array of two or four nontarget letters, demonstrated that peripheral cues captured attention specifically because they were presented with an abrupt onset. While observers searched for the target letter, a new letter suddenly appeared at an empty location, causing a delay in responding to the target. Following these early demonstrations of the special status of onsets with regard to attentional capture, Theeuwes and colleagues (Theeuwes et al., 1998; Theeuwes et al., 1999) showed that abrupt onsets not only capture attention but also capture the eyes. Theeuwes and colleagues developed the so-called oculomotor capture paradigm in which observers are required to make a saccadic eye movement toward the only gray element in the display. On some trials, an irrelevant object was added to the display, and this object was presented with an abrupt onset. The condition in which a new object was added to the display was compared to a control condition in which no sudden onsets were added. When no onset was presented, observers made a saccade directly to the target. However, when an abrupt onset took place, observers made many saccades to the abrupt onset first, before they ultimately ended up at the target location. This erroneous capture of the eyes occurred in about 30–40 percent of the trials (see also Godijn & Theeuwes, 2002). While these studies demonstrated the special status of abrupt onsets in capturing attention, the reason for this special status is still unclear. It may be because onsets are accompanied by luminance transients (see, e.g., Jonides & Yantis, 1988; Theeuwes, 1990, 1994b, 1995; Yantis & Jonides, 1984) or because they represent new objects (e.g., Davoli, Suszko & Abrams, 2007; Franconeri, Hollingworth & Simons, 2005; Yantis & Hillstrom, 1994). Irrespective of the underlying mechanism, it is generally agreed that onsets have the ability to capture attention in a truly bottom-up way.

Initially, it was assumed that bottom-up capture can never be prevented. For example, Jonides (1981) instructed observers to actively ignore the peripheral onset cue, but results showed that capture could not be prevented in spite of the observers trying. Müller and Rabbitt (1989) investigated whether top-down focusing of attention could prevent the capture of attention by abrupt onsets. In their study, a central cue was presented that pointed to a specific location in space. This was followed at different intervals by the presentation of a peripheral box surrounding one of the four possible target locations, which flashed for 50 ms. Even though Müller and Rabbitt found that directing attention to a location in space modulated the extent to which a peripheral flash captured attention, they observed that attention shifted consistently to the location of the onset. Consequently, they concluded that abrupt onsets capture attention in a truly automatic and reflexive way.

However, later studies have shown that top-down attentional control can override bottom-up capture. For example, in Theeuwes (1991b), a central arrowhead was used to instruct observers to direct their attention to one of four placeholders presented equi-spaced in the periphery around the fixation point. After observers directed their attention to one of the locations, an irrelevant abrupt onset was presented at any one of the other locations. Critically, when attention was well focused onto a location in space, abrupt onsets presented elsewhere had no measurable effect on performance. Therefore,

Theeuwes (1991b) concluded that through top-down focusing of spatial attention, bottom-up capture by abrupt onsets can be prevented. Subsequently, it was shown that focusing attention to a location in space can also prevent the capture of the eyes (Theeuwes et al., 1998). Note, however, that the validity of the cue directing attention to a location in space needs to be 100 percent valid. If the cue is not 100 percent valid (but, for example, only 80 percent valid), top-down attentional focusing is not strong enough to prevent capture (e.g., Yantis & Johnston, 1990).

In this respect it is also important to note that preventing attentional capture by abrupt onsets is only possible with a top-down set for a specific location in space but not with a top-down set for focusing attention on a specific nonspatial feature. This was shown by Schreij, Owens and Theeuwes (2008), who instructed observers to search for a unique color singleton and, on some trials, presented an irrelevant abrupt onset shortly after search display onset. While Schreij and colleagues demonstrated cueing effects of the relevant color that clearly established that observers were looking for a particular color, they still found attentional capture by the irrelevant abrupt onset. These findings are at odds with the results from contingent capture studies (Folk et al., 1992) showing that abrupt onsets only capture attention when observers are looking for abrupt onsets (i.e., observers have a top-down set for abrupt onsets), suggesting that attention is never truly captured in a bottom-up way. Even though proponents of the contingent capture hypothesis adhere to the position that abrupt onsets only capture attention when observers are set for them, it is generally assumed that the transient luminance change that accompanies abrupt onsets does trigger a shift of attention that is independent of top-down set (Theeuwes, 2010).

3.2 Bottom-Up Selection by Salient Singletons

As outlined earlier in this Element, abrupt onsets due to luminance transients have the ability to capture attention in a purely bottom-up way. The extent to which static singletons (that have no luminance change) have the ability to capture attention in a purely bottom-up way has been a long-standing controversy in the literature. On one end of the spectrum is the idea that static singletons can capture attention in a purely bottom-up way (Theeuwes, 1991a, 1992, 2010). On the other end is the notion that all selection is basically contingent on the goals and intentions of the observer (Folk et al., 1992) and thus is always under top-down control.

Instrumental in the discussion regarding bottom-up control of attention was once more the additional singleton paradigm that Theeuwes developed in the early nineties (Theeuwes, 1991a, 1992, 1994b). To reiterate, in this paradigm, observers search for one specific and clearly defined salient singleton while another, completely task-irrelevant singleton is simultaneously present. Figure 3 gives an example of a search display from one of the many versions of this paradigm. In this version, observers consistently search for one specific target, for example a green diamond singleton, throughout the entire experiment. In the no-distractor condition, all nontarget elements are green circles and the target (the diamond) is easily selected. In the distractor condition, one of the green circles is colored red, constituting a color distractor singleton. The typical finding is that RT is higher in the condition in which the irrelevant color distractor singleton is present relative to the condition in which no color distractor is present (see Figure 3). It is important to realize that the distractor singleton only causes interference when it is more salient than the target singleton. When it is less salient (see Figure 3; right panels), there is no measurable effect on RT anymore. These findings prompted Theeuwes (1991a, 1992, 1994a, 1994b) to postulate his notion of stimulus-driven capture, arguing that the bottom-up salience signal of the stimuli in visual field determines the selection order. The increase in search time in conditions in

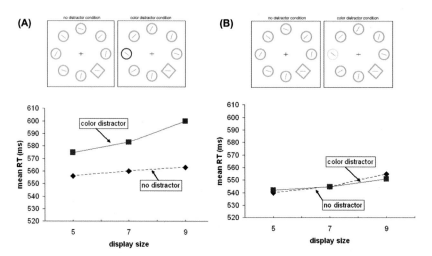

Figure 3 Stimuli and data from Theeuwes (1992). Observers are required to search for a green diamond (target singleton) presented among a variable number of circles and have to respond to the orientation (horizontal or vertical) of the line segment presented within the diamond shape. **(A)** The color distractor singleton captured attention, causing an increase in RT because it was more salient than the target singleton. **(B)** Finding the target singleton is not affected by the presence of the color singleton because the color singleton is less salient than the target singleton (from Theeuwes, 2010) .

which an irrelevant singleton is present was explained in terms of attentional capture.

As the additional singleton task has been used quite extensively over the past twenty-five years or so, it is important to highlight some of its design features. First, the color distractor singleton is never the target so there is no reason for observers to attend to the distractor. If – against the intentions of the observer – this distractor singleton is still selected first, it provides strong evidence for stimulus-driven, bottom-up selection. Yantis and Egeth (1999) pointed out that one can only speak of selection in a purely bottom-up way when the stimulus feature in question is completely task-irrelevant, so that there is no incentive for the observer to attend to it deliberately: "If an object with such an attribute captures attention under these conditions, then and only then can that attribute be said to capture attention in a purely stimulus-driven fashion" (p. 663). Second, when performing the additional singleton task, observers search for a target (e.g., a green diamond) but respond to the orientation of the line segment inside the diamond shape. This has been called a compound search task (Duncan, 1985), which makes it possible to disentangle factors affecting the selection of the target from those affecting the selection of the response. The advantage of this compound search is that the response requirements remain the same over all conditions, ensuring that the RT effects caused by the presence of the color distractor are due to perceptual interference and not to response interference. Third, in the original additional singleton paradigm, the target and distractor singleton were equally likely presented anywhere in the visual field, ensuring that observers are not biased to attend to a particular location. As discussed later in this Element, the paradigm has more recently been used to specifically investigate these attentional biases by presenting the target and/or the distractor more often in one location than in all other locations (Wang & Theeuwes, 2018a, 2018b, 2018c; see Section 4.3). Fourth, in the standard version of the paradigm, the target and distractor singleton are presented simultaneously. This is an important feature because only then does maximum competition take place between target and distractor (Desimone & Duncan, 1995). Consistent with this idea, Mathôt and Theeuwes (2010) found hardly any biased competition between a target and onset distractor singleton when they are presented sequentially. Also, Theeuwes, Atchley and Kramer (2000) showed that the interference effect of a color distractor singleton (as in the additional singleton task of Theeuwes, 1992) is no longer present when the color distractor is presented 150 ms before the target singleton. In other words, by presenting the target and distractor at different moments in time it is possible to create more or less biased competition.

In another often-used variant of the additional singleton paradigm, observers have to search for a unique shape, which can either be a diamond among circles or a circle among diamonds (Theeuwes 1991a). Analogously, if present, the distractor has a unique color, which is either a red element among green elements or a green element among red elements. In other words, in this version, target and distractor features change unpredictably from trial to trial. As can be seen in Figure 4, RT interference effects under these conditions are much larger (about 100–150 ms; see also Pinto, Olivers & Theeuwes, 2005) than in the traditional version of the paradigm. The particular experiment from Theeuwes (1991a) also had another condition in which the distractor was identical to the target. For example, two diamonds appeared among seven circles. One of the diamonds had a vertical or horizontal line segment making it the target, while the other diamond had a 45° or 135° tilted line segment making it the "shape" distractor. Figure 4 shows that this condition gave even larger interference effects (up to 250 ms). The interference in these conditions is so large because, after attention has been captured, it takes substantial time to decide whether the element that has captured attention is the target (which can only be determined on the basis of the orientation of the line segment inside). Only then can attention be shifted away from the distractor element and thus, eventually, to

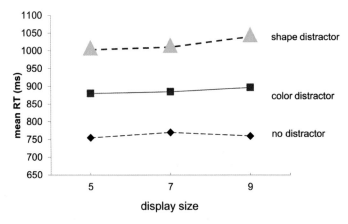

Figure 4 Data from Theeuwes (1991a). Observers searched for a unique shape (either a circle among diamonds or a diamond among circles, randomly mixed within a block) and responded to the orientation (horizontal or vertical) of the line segment presented within the unique shape. A distractor with a unique color (color distractor condition) captured attention and slowed target search for about 120 ms. A distractor with the same shape as the target (shape distractor condition) slowed search even more, causing an interference effect of about 250 ms.

the target. We have shown that this aspect of disengagement of attention from a distractor is very much driven by the similarity between the distractor and the target (Born, Kerzel & Theeuwes, 2011), and others have shown that interference effects can be much larger (e.g., Fockert, Rees, Frith & Lavie 2004). In other words, it is assumed that capture effects are usually small unless uncertainty about the target and distractor requires a relatively long dwell time at the location of the distractor.

As noted, researchers have reached no general agreement on whether salient singletons capture attention in a bottom-up way. The contingent capture hypothesis represents a view that is completely opposite of the bottom-up capture account (Folk et al., 1992). The evidence for this account comes from studies using a cueing task in which observers have to ignore a "cue" presented just before the search display. When the search display was preceded by a to-be-ignored featural singleton (the "cue") that matched the singleton for which observers were searching, the cue captured attention, as evidenced by a prolonged reaction time to identify the target (i.e., when the cue and target appeared in different spatial locations). However, if the to-be-ignored featural singleton cue did not match the singleton for which observers were looking, its presentation had no measurable effect on responding, which suggests that observers completely ignored this irrelevant singleton cue. In other words, if the cue did not match the top-down search goal (i.e., the defining property of the target), then there was no effect on RT (i.e., a null effect). Yet, when the cue matched the search goal, it affected RT. For example, when observers were looking for a color singleton target, they completely ignored an abrupt onset cue presented just before the search display. Even though the results of this paradigm have been interpreted as evidence that selection is always top down (and therefore never bottom up), it became more evident in recent years that the results of this paradigm may be much more easily explained in terms of intertrial priming and/or selection history (see Section 4.1).

4 Selection History

A few years back, Awh and colleagues (2012) proposed that the view which has dominated the field for the past thirty years is insufficient. Instead of considering selection as only a result of the interaction between top-down and bottom-up processes, they argued that many instances of selection are driven by previous selection experiences (i.e., selection history) that have nothing to do with goal-driven or stimulus-driven factors (see also Failing & Theeuwes, 2018; Theeuwes, 2018, 2019). A key factor in this discussion is that selection is in many instances driven neither by the goals of the observer nor by the salient properties of the environment. Instead, attentional biases may develop through experience.

Many examples demonstrate how previous selection experiences affect current selection priorities. For example, scenes from everyday life contain semantic regularities that dramatically affect the way we search and find objects. In the early 1970s, Biederman (1972) demonstrated that objects violating the regularities learned over a lifetime are more difficult to find, for example, when presented at inconsistent (unusual) locations within a scene. Similarly, objects that appear in an inconsistent scene context (e.g., a bicycle in a kitchen scene) are more difficult to identify (e.g., Biederman, Mezzanotte & Rabinowitz, 1982). Võ and Wolfe (2013) refined this work and made a distinction between semantic and syntactic scene-object relationships, referring to the type of objects and where these objects are likely to be found within a scene. For example, a coffeemaker, pan and knife are likely to co-occur in a kitchen scene, and within that scene they are likely to occur in particular places (on the stove, and less likely on the ground).

It is well known that selection experiences play a large role in skilled and complex tasks such as navigating in traffic by car or by bicycle. Indeed, because the road environment is visually complex, in many circumstances, selection depends very much on acquired expectations learned over a lifetime. In other words, drivers will perceive events that are in line with their expectations and will overlook those that are not. For example, a pedestrian walking along a highway is difficult to detect because pedestrians are usually not seen on highways. Typically, collisions occur because drivers did not expect particular events to happen and thus did not anticipate appropriate behavior adequately. The fact that accident data show that most accidents are the result of drivers simply overlooking clearly visible objects indicates that these acquired expectations do play a large role (Sussman, Bishop, Madnick & Walter, 1985). Experienced drivers have learned to expect particular road elements (e.g., signs, lights or markings) and particular road users (e.g., cars, bikes or pedestrians) to appear at particular locations within specific road environments (e.g., highways, rural roads or city roads; see Theeuwes & Godthelp, 1995; Theeuwes, Van der Horst & Kuiken, 2012).

The underlying notion of what is meant by selection history is that through (explicit or implicit) learning (i.e., processes shaped by past episodes of attentional selection), particular stimuli may receive "value" that affects future selection episodes above and beyond top-down and bottom-up factors. Currently, three broad classes of phenomena related to lingering biases due to selection history have been identified (see Failing & Theeuwes, 2018).

4.1 Priming

One widely known influence of memory processes on attentional selection is priming, which describes how a stimulus (feature) repeatedly attended to in the recent past is more efficiently selected and identified on the current trial (Maljkovic & Nakayama, 1994; Tulving & Schacter, 1990). In a series of now classic experiments, Maljkovic and Nakayama (1994) first demonstrated the influence of priming in the context of a search task (see also Hillstrom, 2000; Olivers & Humphreys, 2003). In their task, observers had to search for a salient shape (e.g., a red diamond among green diamonds) and identify whether the left or the right side of the diamond was cut off (see also Bravo & Nakayama, 1992). They found feature priming between trials: observers were faster when the target color was the same on two consecutive trials compared to when it was swapped. This priming of pop-out, also referred to as intertrial priming, occurred for up to eight successive trials in covert but also overt search (McPeek, Maljkovic & Nakayama, 1999). It even occurred when observers were unaware of repetitions (Maljkovic & Nakayama, 2000), or when they were explicitly informed that the target was unlikely to be the same between trials (Maljkovic & Nakayama, 1994). Overall, priming is now considered to have a low-level facilitatory effect on perceptual processing and is determined by traces of past selection history (Kristjánsson, 2010; Kristjánsson & Campana, 2010; Lamy & Kristjánsson, 2013; Theeuwes, 2013; Theeuwes, Reimann & Mortier, 2006; Theeuwes & Van der Burg, 2007, 2011).

Scholars generally agree that priming is an automatic process that takes place without any intent and cannot be counteracted even if observers try to do so. Hickey, Chelazzi and Theeuwes (2010) demonstrated this in a reward priming study using a variant of the additional singleton paradigm. In this study, observers could receive a high reward after selecting the shape singleton target. When the target happened to be of the same color on the next trial, they were faster compared to when the color of the target changed – an effect attributed to intertrial priming. Crucially however, in a follow-up experiment, observers were instructed that whenever a high reward was received, the colors associated with the target would switch. In other words, if the target was red and observers received a high reward, they knew that in 80 percent of the trials, the color of the target on the next trial would be green. Even though it was detrimental to search and reduced actual reward payout, observers could not switch their color set: they remained biased toward the selected color that had garnered them a high reward on the previous trial even though they knew it would have been beneficial to switch to the other color.

This study shows that priming causes a bias that cannot be counteracted in a top-down volitional way: observers kept selecting the color selected on the previous trial even though it was detrimental for their performance. A study by Theeuwes and Van der Burg (2013) may explain why this effect persisted. In two experiments, Theeuwes and Van der Burg had observers perform either a temporal order judgment task (TOJ) or a simultaneity judgment task (SJ) to indicate which of two equally salient but differently colored test stimuli was presented first. The two test stimuli were presented lateralized at different stimulus onset asynchronies (SOA) and their onset was preceded by a centrally presented stimulus colored in one of the two test stimuli colors. Both tasks measured the so-called prior entry effect, which is thought to be a bias-free indication of which stimulus is perceived first. The results showed that stimuli whose features were identical to those of the centrally presented stimulus were perceived to appear earlier in time than stimuli with other features. Van der Burg and Theeuwes argued that the central stimulus primed certain features that caused them to become subjectively more salient such that their processing was accelerated, leading to prior entry into awareness.

The role of priming in attentional selection was also demonstrated in another study by Theeuwes and Van der Burg (2011). In this study, observers viewed displays in which two salient singletons were simultaneously presented (e.g., a red and green target circle among a number of grey circles; see Figure 5). Each of the circles enclosed either a vertical or horizontal line segment and observers were required to respond to the orientation of the line segment. Before the search display was presented, observers received a cue that indicated which circle had to be selected in the upcoming trial. This cue was a simple word saying "red," "green" – that is, whatever color the target was on the next upcoming trial. The time interval between word cue and search display was relatively long (about 1.5 s) to ensure that observers could optimally set their top-down set for the color that needed to be selected on the upcoming trial. The cue was also 100 percent valid to give the maximum incentive to the observer to make use of the cue. In principle, this approach is very similar to a Posner cueing task in which observers need to prepare for the location for an upcoming target. The goal of this study was to test whether observers can prepare themselves for a specific feature (i.e., prepare for a specific color). The assumption was that through the top-down set, observers should be able to selectively increase the weight of the relevant feature of the target on the upcoming trial. If the weight of the feature can be enhanced in a top-down way, one expects that selection becomes biased toward this feature only.

To determine whether selection was efficient, Theeuwes and Van der Burg (2011) made use of a technique known as the "the identity intrusion technique"

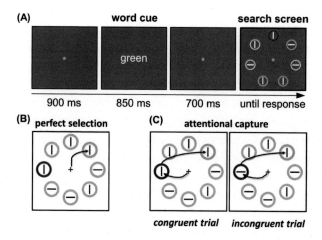

Figure 5 Trial sequence of Theeuwes and van der Burg (2011; top) and hypothetical selection mechanisms (bottom). **(A)** Observers search for the color singleton indicated by the word cue and respond to the line inside of it (here: search for green and respond "vertical"). **(B)** Perfect selection: observers direct attention only to the green singleton and respond to the line segment. **(C)** Imperfect selection: on a subset of trials, attention is captured by the irrelevant red singleton. The line inside the irrelevant distractor singleton can be congruent (e.g., both vertical) or incongruent (e.g., one horizontal and one vertical) with the orientation of the line segment inside the (cued) target singleton. If a congruency effect is found, one can only conclude that at some point before responding, attention was directed to the irrelevant singleton (figure adapted from Theeuwes & Van der Burg, 2011).

first introduced by Theeuwes and Burger (1998). The idea is that if observers are perfectly able to select the target singleton in the color indicated by the cue and respond to the line segment inside of it, then the orientation of the line segment positioned in the distractor singleton (the other pop-out element) should not matter and should not affect responding (Figure 5b). If, however, selection is not perfect, one expects that, at least on a subset of trials, attention will be captured by the distractor singleton before attention is directed to the target singleton. If that is the case, then one expects a congruency effect, which implies that if the line segment inside the distractor singleton is the same as the line inside the target singleton (i.e., congruent), observers respond faster than when the line segments are incongruent (e.g., a horizontal line segment inside the target singleton and a vertical line segment in the distractor singleton) (Figure 5c; see Schreij et al., 2008; Schreij, Theeuwes & Olivers, 2010; Theeuwes, 1995; Theeuwes & Burger, 1998, who applied the same technique).

The results showed a clear congruency effect, indicating that selection was not perfect but instead that, at least in a subset of trials, attention was erroneously directed toward the irrelevant color singleton before it was directed to the target singleton. Theeuwes and Van der Burg concluded that top-down, feature-based selection is limited. Even though all five colors used in this experiment had the same physical saliency (no reliable difference appeared in the absolute RTs between the various colors), observers could not selectively increase the selection weights of the color that was relevant for the upcoming trial in a top-down manner. Crucial for the current discussion on priming was that perfect selection was found (no congruency effect whatsoever) when the color of the previous trial was repeated on the current trial. In other words, if observers selected the red singleton on the preceding (n−1) trial, they could select the red singleton again on the next (n−th) trial without any interference from the irrelevant salient singleton. This demonstrates the role of priming as a major driver of attentional selection.

Theeuwes recently suggested that the influence of priming on selection is often underestimated and erroneously attributed to top-down volitional control (see Theeuwes, 2013, 2018, 2019). For example, on the basis of classic work by Treisman (1988), researchers generally conclude that it is important to know what target dimension one is searching for in a pop-out search – that is, whether one is searching for a color or a shape singleton. This conclusion is based on the finding that observers are typically 100 ms faster when they search for a specific singleton (e.g., a color singleton) throughout a whole block of trials ("blocked" condition) relative to when they have to search for one of two different singletons (e.g., a color and a shape singleton) in a whole block of trials ("mixed" condition). The idea is that observers cannot have a top-down set for the target they are looking for in mixed blocks. Because they do not know the search template (e.g., a color singleton) in this condition, search is slower compared to when they do know the template in the blocked condition. These findings are traditionally interpreted as evidence for top-down search of feature dimensions (see Found & Müller, 1996; Kumada, 1999; Müller, Heller & Ziegler, 1995; Wolfe et al., 2003). Clearly, given the foregoing discussion, it appears that these effects may have nothing to do with top-down knowledge about the target. Instead, they may simply be due to massive intertrial priming occurring in the blocked condition in which observers continuously search for the same target over the course of an entire block.

In a similar vein, the notion of contingent capture (e.g., Folk et al., 1992) can also be considered to be the result of priming. To reiterate, the contingent capture hypothesis states that, at any given time, selection of a particular stimulus feature critically depends on the perceptual goals held by the observer.

In this respect, the contingent capture hypothesis assumes a dominant role for top-down control. However, one aspect in the design of contingent capture studies has been greatly overlooked: in basically all studies, observers are required to search for a particular target feature throughout a whole block of trials. In other words, in all these experiments, strong intertrial priming occurs because the target remains the same across an entire block of trials. If it is really about the top-down set at any given time, one should be able to flexibly switch the top-down set from trial to trial. Varying the target-defining features from trial to trial would prevent intertrial priming. Belopolsky, Schreij and Theeuwes (2010) conducted such an experiment using the classic contingent capture paradigm. Instead of keeping the target fixed across a whole block of trial, they varied the target that needed to be searched for randomly from trial to trial: observers were instructed to search for one or the other target (e.g., search for an onset, or search for a color). The results showed no evidence whatsoever for contingent capture. Regardless of which target observers were searching for, the salient cue captured attention. In other words, the classic contingent capture effect that has been considered to be a prime example of how the top-down set affects selection is no longer present when target features vary. Thus, it appears that it can be more easily explained in terms of intertrial priming. Note, however, that recent studies have shown that intertrial priming cannot explain all aspects of contingent capture (Ansorge, Kiss, Worschech & Eimer, 2011; Kerzel & Witzel, 2019; Schoeberl, Goller & Ansorge, 2019).

At this point, it is important to emphasize that perceptual priming – as one of the examples of how selection history biases attentional selection – should not be mistaken for what has been called response priming, which is a selection bias that is the result of the buildup of automatic associations between stimuli and response tendencies. In all priming studies discussed earlier in this Element, the response of the observer is unrelated to what they are searching for. In this sense, priming represents the efficiency with which the target can be selected; not the speed with which the response can be emitted (see Theeuwes & Van der Burg, 2007, 2011).

4.2 Reward

As we have argued in the previous section, priming is one of the ways by which past selection can influence current selection. The recent years have provided mounting evidence that responses to stimuli that have led to rewarding experiences in the past have a large effect on attentional selection (for reviews, see Anderson, 2013, 2016a; Chelazzi, Perlato, Santandrea & Della Libera, 2013; Failing & Theeuwes, 2018; Le Pelley, Mitchell, Beesley, George & Wills, 2016;

Vuilleumier, 2015). However, before going into detail regarding this class of selection history effects, it is important to distinguish between two ways by which reward can affect selection. On the one hand, reward may act as an incentive to motivate particular behavior. In other words, observers may exert more effort (i.e., "work harder") at a particular task because they expect to be rewarded for it. This type of reward influence has been shown to have a nonspecific or general effect on attentional selection that is directly tied to immediate reward expectations. In that sense, this influence is very much strategic and thus considered to be top-down in origin. Although important, a detailed discussion of this aspect is beyond the scope of this Element (see Failing & Theeuwes, 2018, for a more detailed discussion). More important to the current discussion is the mounting evidence that reward delivery shapes selection behavior by inducing biases that continue to affect selection even when selection is no longer rewarded and even when these biases counteract the goals of the observer. In essence, this influence is another example of how selection history has a persistent influence on ongoing selection that cannot be explained in terms of top-down or bottom-up processes alone. In what follows, we describe several ways how reward can create what we consider reward-based selection history.

4.2.1 Value-Driven Attentional Capture and Other Persistent Selection Biases Due to Reward

Among the first to demonstrate persistent biases in attentional selection due to reward were Della Libera and colleagues (Della Libera & Chelazzi, 2006, 2009; Della Libera, Perlato & Chelazzi, 2011). For example, in one study, Della Libera and Chelazzi (2009) tested observers on two separate occasions over the course of five days. These two sessions, or a training and test session, were specifically designed to investigate whether the influence of reward on selection would persist for an extended period of time even when reward could no longer be earned. To this end, observers were rewarded for successfully matching shapes during the extensive training session. The crucial manipulation was that reward payout was biased toward specific relationships of a given shape and its role in the search task (i.e., whether it was a target or a distractor). Observers received a high reward when certain shapes appeared as targets, while other shapes garnered observers a low reward when they appeared as targets. Likewise, yet other shapes were associated with a high reward when they appeared as distractors, while others were associated with a low reward when they appeared as distractors. Whenever a shape appeared in a different role than its predefined role, reward payout was equally often a high or a low reward. Yet in spite of this systematic manipulation, observers were told that reward payout on any given trial depended on their performance (i.e., how accurately and quickly they responded). In the subsequent test session, during which observers performed an almost identical task but could no longer earn any reward, Della Libera and Chelazzi found that performance was still affected by the relationships learned during the training session: (i) Test phase distractor shapes that had to be ignored in order to earn a high reward during the training led to faster RT relative to when the distractor shapes were associated with low reward during training. (ii) Test phase distractor shapes that functioned as high reward–associated targets during training slowed reaction time significantly relative to when these distractor shapes were low reward–associated targets during training. These findings provided the first clear evidence that the administration of reward during training has an effect on how the visual system continues to process the stimuli that previously had a consistent relationship with reward. According to the authors, a stimulus can thus become a potent distractor when one has a history of being rewarded for selecting it even if that reward is no longer delivered. Conversely, when receiving a reward for successfully ignoring a stimulus, such stimuli may become much harder to select even when one no longer receives reward. In other words, past reward experiences shape the level of priority for attentional selection by either facilitating or inhibiting selection of certain stimuli long after learning has been completed and reward has ceased to be delivered. Moreover, by finding these effects up to five days following the training, the findings by Della Libera and colleagues also demonstrate that the influence of reward is not limited to the time immediately following the trial and thus is not merely a consequence of intertrial reward priming.

Although these findings were important, they also raised several questions regarding the true nature of the underlying reward bias. More specifically, one may wonder how far these effects are the consequence of selection history instead of top-down processes (in particular task relevance) since all stimuli were equally often presented as distractors and targets during the training as well as the test session. Second, it was unclear whether the influence of reward affected initial stimulus selection (i.e., attentional capture) or whether it was more difficult for observers to disengage attention from reward-associated stimuli. Finally, only when the training and test sessions were identical did the reward-associated distractors interfere with target selection, which brings into question the generalizability of these findings (cf. Experiments 1 and 2 in Della Libera & Chelazzi, 2009).

In another line of research, Anderson and colleagues (Anderson, Laurent & Yantis, 2011) directly addressed some of these questions. In their experiments, they also made use of a training and a test session. In the training session, observers performed a color search task, covertly searching for either a red or a green outline shape among differently colored shapes. For accurate and quick performance on reporting the orientation of a line segment placed inside the target shape observers received reward. Unbeknownst to the observers, the magnitude of reward was associated with the color of the target (probabilistically high or low or 80/20 for one color and 20/80 for the other). For example, for one observer, green targets were associated with a high reward and red targets were associated with a low reward. Following the training, observers performed a variant of the additional singleton search task (Theeuwes, 1992) in which they had to search for a colored shape singleton presented among randomly colored nontarget shapes. During this test session, they could no longer earn reward. In contrast to the classic additional singleton task in which the distractor is a physically salient element, Anderson and colleagues used the previous target colors as non-salient distractors. Depending on the condition, this distractor could be either the high reward (e.g., green) or the low reward (e.g., red) target from the training session. The results showed that, relative to a distractor absent condition, this distractor interfered with target search even though it was physically non-salient. Interference in target search was observed although color information was not even part of the task set, although observers were explicitly informed to ignore any color information, and were told that the target color was never one of the two distractor colors. This demonstrates that reward had a persistent influence on how these colors were processed. The authors concluded that these results suggest that the stimulus associated with high reward captured attention during the reward-free test session in a way that cannot be explained in terms of bottom-up or top-down processes. However, since both distractor conditions (high and low reward) were only compared to a distractor-free condition, it was unclear how far the distractor effects were truly the result of reward-based selection history. Indeed, Anderson and colleagues (2011) reported no reliable difference between the high- and low-reward distractor conditions (although a later reanalysis of the data and replication of the study did find this difference; Anderson & Halpern, 2017, but see Grubb & Li, 2018). This implies the existence of differences in the magnitude of reward associated with target selection and differences in the number of times targets were selected during training. In other words, differences emerged in the reward delivered during training *and* differences in selection history. Moreover, it was unclear whether these effects were truly the consequence of spatial attentional capture by reward-associated stimuli.

Following this pioneering work of Anderson and colleagues, other studies provided more conclusive evidence for the capture of spatial attention by previously reward-associated stimuli. Failing and Theeuwes (2014) demonstrated performance costs and benefits of stimuli previously associated with reward using a variant of Posner's spatial cueing experiment (Posner & Cohen, 1984; Posner, Snyder & Davidson, 1980). Finding such costs and benefits is considered direct evidence for shifts of spatial attention thereby precluding alternative explanations of distractor interference due to, for example, nonspatial filtering costs (Kahneman, Treisman & Burkell, 1983). In their experiment, participants had to search for a target letter enclosed by a colored circle during a separate training and test session. Two elements were always on display, one on each side of fixation. The results of the test session showed that attention was consistently oriented toward the circle that had a color associated with reward during training. If this circle contained the target letter, participants responded faster than the baseline, which consisted of two circles having colors that had neither been preferentially selected nor rewarded during training. If the circle did not contain the target letter, attention needed to be reoriented away from it, causing significant costs relative to baseline. Converging evidence for the idea that the specific reward associations learned during training had induced the persistent changes in how the reward-associated stimuli are selected, Failing and Theeuwes (2014) also found that a larger reward during learning (i.e., facilitated selection of the reward-associated target during training) was positively correlated with larger selection costs (i.e., attentional capture) of the reward-associated stimuli during the test session. In short, this study provided the first direct evidence for capture due to reward-based selection history rather than selection history per se by keeping selection history constant while varying reward history. In another study, Theeuwes and Belopolsky (2012) used a variant of the oculomotor capture task (Theeuwes et al., 1998) and demonstrated that eye movements are affected by reward-based selection history in a very similar way. They found that observers made more erroneous saccades to an abrupt onset stimulus during a reward-free test session if the color of that onset stimulus was previously associated with a high reward compared to when it was associated with a low reward during the training session (see also Anderson & Yantis, 2012; Bucker, Silvis, Donk & Theeuwes, 2015).

Other experiments showed that the influence of reward-based selection history is not constrained to spatial shifts of attention but also affects the deployment of attention across time. In an adaption of the very influential attentional blink paradigm (AB; Raymond, Shapiro & Arnell, 1992), Raymond and O'Brien (2009) showed – for the first time – that reward influenced temporal selection. In the classic AB experiment, a series of stimuli such as letters, digits or pictures are presented in rapid succession (6–20 items per second) at a single location in space. The task of the observer is to detect or discriminate between the features of two target stimuli, which are embedded at different positions in the stream. The typical finding is that performance on the second target is significantly worse when it is presented shortly (200 ms) after the first target compared to when the time interval is longer (e.g., 800 ms or more; Dux & Marois, 2009; Shapiro, Raymond & Arnell, 1997). Since the spatial location of the target is certain but the time point at which it is present is not, the AB is a powerful tool to uncover the limits of attention across time.

Like the previous studies on the persistence of reward-based selection history, Raymond and O'Brien (2009) made use of two separate experimental sessions. During the training session, observers could earn monetary reward by choosing one of two face stimuli on a given trial. Different face stimuli were associated with winning, losing or neither winning nor losing reward (i.e., baseline condition). In the subsequent reward-free test session, observers performed a variant of the AB task in which they were always shown two targets (T1 and T2). The presentation of both targets was separated by either a long or a short interval. In one experiment, T1 was a patch of circles or squares and T2 was either a face shown during training or a new (unseen) face. Observers simply had to discriminate between circles and squares on T1 and old or new face pictures on T2. The results showed that the recognition of the face stimuli seen earlier depended on the expected value associated with them during training: faces previously associated with winning were more often recognized compared to faces associated with neither winning nor losing reward. Importantly though, all faces except those associated with winning reward showed the classic AB (i.e., impaired performance on face recognition of T2 when both targets are separated by a short interval). Conversely, in a follow-up experiment where the order of target stimuli was swapped such that T1 was a face stimulus and T2 the patch with either circles or lines, faces previously associated with winning reward were still recognized more reliably, yet they also elicited a reliable AB. This pattern of results led Raymond and O'Brien (2009) to conclude that associating a stimulus with reward leads to a persistent change in how well these stimuli are recognized and, crucially, that this change causes such stimuli to overcome the AB.

Overcoming the AB by means of associating reward is an important finding and fits well with other evidence suggesting that associating reward with a stimulus modulates the attentional priority of that stimulus. However, finding that recognition of T2 is unaffected by the reward association of T1 is somewhat puzzling given that a change in attentional priority of T1 should come at the expense of other stimuli (including physically more salient targets). In particular, the AB effect has been suggested to be the consequence of failed attentional suppression during T1 processing (Martens & Wyble, 2010; Taatgen, Juvina, Schipper, Borst & Martens, 2009; Wyble, Bowman & Nieuwenstein, 2009).

In another study, Failing and Theeuwes (2015) suggested that Raymond and O'Brien (2009) had not observed any interference in T2 performance because the attentional processing of T2 was already at maximum priority. After all, the T2 stimulus was a target and task relevant throughout the entire test session. Therefore, Failing and Theeuwes (2015) conducted experiments in which the reward-associated stimulus was always a task-irrelevant stimulus during the test session. And indeed, when occasionally presenting previously reward-associated stimuli as distractors during the test session, the sensitivity in detecting a single target in a stream of briefly presented stimuli suffered. The strongest interference in target detection was observed when the distractor that was associated with the relatively largest reward was present. A particularly interesting aspect of this study was that the reward was associated with the semantic content of complex visual scenes and that the persistent effect of reward was observed even if new, unseen pictures with the same semantic content were used during the test session of a follow-up experiment (Failing & Theeuwes, 2015, Experiment 2). Since the stimuli in the AB task are only shown very briefly, this suggests that reward can either be associated with the complex set of features that are common for a given semantic content or may act on the level of gist perception. Together, these studies (Failing & Theeuwes, 2015; Le Pelley, Seabrooke, Kennedy, Pearson & Most, 2017; Le Pelley, Watson, Pearson, Abeywickrama & Most, 2018; Raymond & O'Brien, 2009) show that persistent changes in attentional priority due to reward associations extend to temporal attentional selection.

By now there is overwhelming behavioral evidence from covert and overt attention studies for what is commonly referred to as value-driven attentional capture (VDAC). Evidence for this phenomenon ranges from reward-based selection history affecting selection of low-level features up to more complex stimuli like faces, objects or entire visual scenes. Reward has been shown to affect feature-specific as well as spatially specific processing (Anderson & Kim, 2019; Chelazzi et al., 2014; Hickey, Chelazzi & Theeuwes, 2014), although the specific circumstances under which each of them is affected are still unclear (Jiang, Li & Remington, 2015; Won & Leber, 2016). Reward-based selection history affects contextual cueing (Pollmann, Eštočinová, Sommer, Chelazzi & Zinke, 2016; Tseng & Lleras, 2013) and processing in the temporal (Failing, & Theeuwes, 2016; Hickey & Los, 2015; Rajsic, Perera & Pratt, 2016) as well as in the auditory domain (Asutay & Västfjäll, 2016). Evidence from studies with patient populations as well as populations from different stages of development furthermore suggest that the extent to which individuals exhibit this attentional bias differs depending on age or psychopathologies (e.g., Anderson, Kronemer, Rilee, Sacktor & Marvel, 2016; Anderson, Leal, Hall, Yassa & Yantis, 2014; Roper, Vecera & Vaidya, 2014).

Although fewer studies have investigated the influence of reward-based selection history on attention in the brain, those that have support the conclusions drawn in the behavioral or eye-tracking studies. Indeed, electrophysiological studies using training and test session designs to investigate the persistent effects of reward associations on attention provide evidence for modulations in attentional as well as perceptual processing. For example, Qi and colleagues (Qi, Zeng, Ding & Li, 2013) found a larger N2pc component for distractors previously associated with a high reward during a reward-free test session. In line with the idea that distraction by a reward-associated distractor could only be overcome if observers could suppress the distractor, Qi and colleagues also observed a larger P_D component, but only for the high-reward distractor in trials with low reaction times (see also Feldmann-Wüstefeld & Schubö, 2016). Conversely, there was no modulation of the N2pc in these trials. While these results support the conclusion that attentional priority is increased such that the reward-associated stimulus is either erroneously selected (indexed by the N2pc, which represents the shift of attention) or has to be suppressed (indexed by the P_D), another study also showed altered perceptual processing of a reward-associated stimulus up to seven days after the reward learning phase. Indeed, MacLean and Giesbrecht (2015) found that reward-associated stimuli elicited a larger P1, which is a component assumed to reflect early visual processing in the extrastriate cortex without any attentional modulation (Hillyard, Vogel & Luck, 1998; Luck & Hillyard, 1994).

The evidence for changes in attentional processing of previously reward-associated stimuli from electrophysiological studies is also supported by neuroimaging studies. Early studies observed changes in the neuronal representations of stimuli associated with reward, such that targets associated with reward were more strongly represented in early visual cortex (Serences, 2008; Serences & Saproo, 2010). More recently, it was also shown that representations of distractor objects associated with reward were suppressed in the object-selective cortex compared to before they were associated with reward (Hickey & Peelen, 2015). This is consistent with the idea that the reward association required the suppression of the distractor in order to prevent its interference with target search. In a similar vein, quite a few VDAC studies have found activity in areas typically associated with changes in spatial selection priority. Anderson and colleagues (Anderson, 2016b; Anderson, Laurent & Yantis, 2014), for example, demonstrated that previously reward-associated stimuli evoked activity in extrastriate cortex and the intraparietal sulcus (IPS), which are considered to be critically involved in attentional control (Serences et al., 2005). More specifically, the IPS has frequently been suggested to be the site of a spatial priority map for attentional selection, which suggests that the previously reward-associated stimulus continues to compete for attention at higher levels of the selection process even when reward is no longer delivered.

Besides the involvement of brain structures along the ventral and dorsal streams typically considered to play an important role in visual attention and perception, there is also considerable evidence for the involvement of the dorsal striatum, particularly the tail of the caudate nucleus. In primates, neurons in the caudate tail have been shown to receive information from the ventral visual pathway (Yeterian & Van Hoesen, 1978) and to contain information regarding the location and identity of target objects currently associated with reward value (Yamamoto, Monosov, Yasuda & Hikosaka, 2012). Yet VDAC studies suggest that the caudate tail is also active when previously reward-associated stimuli have become distractors that are no longer associated with any reward (Anderson et al., 2016; Anderson et al., 2014). Besides the representation of stable value associations (Kim & Hikosaka, 2013; Hikosaka, Kim, Yasuda & Yamamoto, 2014), the function of this activity in the context of this task is not immediately clear. On the one hand, the caudate formation has been shown to be sensitive to particularly spatial information (Hikosaka et al., 2014; Postle & D'Esposito, 1999, 2003; Yamamoto et al., 2012), which might indicate that activity in this area also reflects the coding of spatial information of the reward-associated stimulus that eventually get propagated to the priority map of attentional selection elsewhere in the brain. On the other hand, the caudate formation is also highly innervated by dopamine neurons, which are widely thought to represent reward prediction error signals that track the updating of value associations (e.g., Schultz, 2016; but see Berridge & Robinson, 1998; Berridge, Robinson & Aldridge, 2009). Thus, it may be that this signal is the neuronal footprint of updating the reward prediction error signals induced by the reward feedback, or rather the lack of reward feedback, during the extinction of the reward association (i.e., test phase). This latter explanation seems particularly feasible given the evidence from the only VDAC study that measured dopamine during the test phase (Anderson et al., 2016). Here, a correlation between the release of dopamine in the right anterior and posterior caudate and the distractive capability of the previously reward-associated distractor was found only during the first epoch of the test phase.

4.2.2 Reward-Based Attentional Bias via Pavlovian Reward Learning

While VDAC studies have provided tremendous insight into the influence of reward-based selection history on current attentional selection, the defining design feature of these studies also constitutes a weakness concerning some of the conclusions that can be drawn. In an attempt to disentangle the influence of immediate reward feedback from persistent influence of past reward learning, these studies split the experiment up into a training and test session. Importantly, during the training sessions, the reward-associated stimuli always had instrumental value. In terms of the terminology of attentional control, these stimuli were always task relevant during training because they were the stimuli observers had to attend and respond to, and only if they did so accurately and quickly enough would they earn reward. In this sense, prioritizing selection of a previously reward-associated stimulus during training was an instrumentally conditioned response (Thorndike, 1911) or habitual attention response (Anderson, 2016a; Le Pelley et al., 2016) that was carried into the test session. On the basis of these studies, it therefore remains unclear whether the underlying associative mechanism is merely instrumental conditioning or can (also) be Pavlovian conditioning. In Pavlovian conditioning, a stimulus that is associated with reward and that eventually affects biases attention may only have signaling value, but its selection itself is neither necessary nor sufficient for reward delivery.

Other studies set out to investigate whether reward-based selection occurs exclusively due to the establishment of an instrumental relationship with a specific stimulus or instead can also be the consequence of a Pavlovian relationship. One of the first studies to address this question ensured that reward delivery and task relevance were independent of each other throughout the entire experiment (Peck, Jangraw, Suzuki, Efem & Gottlieb, 2009). In this primate study, monkeys received reward depending on a reward-signaling cue shown prior to the onset of target. Importantly, although the reward cues were presented in the same two locations as the target and the distractor, on any given trial the cues were not predictive of the target location. Moreover, in order to earn reward, the reward cues could be entirely ignored since only the selection of the target would result in reward delivery. In spite of that, Peck and colleagues observed that the monkeys' eye movements were biased toward the reward-signaling cues. They also observed that the neuronal firing rate in the lateral intraparietal cortex (LIP), the monkey analog of the human IPS, was elevated for cues that reliably predicted reward delivery. This is consistent with the idea that the representation of a reward-associated stimulus is altered by reward learning and that this alteration is reflected in increased selection priority. Although an important finding, this design presented a few shortcomings with respect to the interpretation in terms of reward-based selection history due to Pavlovian learning. One regards the training procedure prior to data collection. Monkeys are typically trained extensively (across months) to learn to perform the task. The training involves the almost exclusive delivery of the same primary rewards that will be administered during the data collection phase. The extent to which one can claim that there is no instrumental relationship between the stimuli used in the task is therefore unclear. Since the reward-associated and target stimuli were presented in temporal succession rather than at the same time, it is furthermore unclear whether the reward-associated stimulus directly competes with the target stimulus for attentional selection. It may be that it had only received selection priority because it had been presented ahead of the target.

More recent studies by Le Pelley and colleagues aimed to address such shortcomings by investigating whether competition for attentional selection occurs from an entirely task-irrelevant but reward-signaling stimulus that never coincides with the target location on a given trial and whose selection never directly results in reward (Le Pelley, Pearson, Griffiths & Beesley, 2015; Pearson, Donkin, Tran, Most & Le Pelley, 2015; see Experiment 2 in Mine & Saiki, 2015, for a conceptually similar approach in the context of a training-test session paradigm). One crucial difference to previous studies is that selecting the reward-signaling cue would come at a cost equivalent to impaired task performance and reduced reward payout throughout the entire experiment. To this end, they made use of a variant of the additional singleton task (Theeuwes, 1992). Observers searched for a shape singleton and were required to indicate the orientation of a line segment appearing in that singleton. On a subset of trials, a color distractor singleton was present. This distractor was associated with the monetary reward that would be paid out for a correct and quick response on that trial. One color (e.g., red) was associated with a high reward, while another color (e.g., green) was associated with a low reward. An important design feature was that even though the distractor signaled reward, the best strategy to earn that reward was to simply ignore it. In fact, Le Pelley and colleagues imposed a flexible time limit on the task to ensure that attending the reward-signaling stimulus would come at a cost at any point in the experiment. If observers exceeded this consistently adjusted time limit, they would no longer receive reward for accurate responses. Yet in spite of these manipulations, observers were significantly slower in searching the target when the distractor was associated with a high reward compared to when it was associated with a low reward. In other words, even though the distractor was never task relevant or its selection in any way beneficial it demanded attention, distracting observers away from the target. In a follow-up experiment, Le Pelley and colleagues demonstrated similar effects on eye movement behavior by showing that observers would look more often at the distractor signaling high reward even when that would lead to the omission of reward (Le Pelley et al.,

2015). The authors argued that this provided strong evidence for involuntary capture by reward-signaling distractors through Pavlovian associative learning.

Although convincing, these experiments have an important caveat regarding the conclusion that attention is solely biased due to Pavlovian associative learning. Different to VDAC studies, the stimuli associated with reward were also physically salient throughout the entire experiment. As we discussed earlier, physically salient stimuli are known to elicit automatic, involuntary capture of attention. The crucial question is whether stimuli that are physically not salient (and therefore do not capture attention) can acquire capturing qualities when associated with reward. To address this drawback, Failing and colleagues (Failing, Nissens, Pearson, Le Pelley & Theeuwes, 2015; Failing & Theeuwes, 2017; see also Bucker, Belopolsky & Theeuwes, 2015) developed a procedure in which the reward-signaling distractor was never task relevant and also never physically salient (see Figure 6). Yet in spite of the important change in the experimental procedure, they also found that observers' eyes were captured by a stimulus signaling relatively high reward. Interestingly, they also observed that capture was particularly pronounced in early first saccades (i.e., initial saccades with a short onset time). This is typically taken as evidence for involuntary biases that influence eye movements prior to the exertion of top-down control.

In light of these studies, it is important to briefly discuss the role of explicit knowledge. Some studies explicitly informed observers about the relationship of the stimulus and reward (Failing & Theeuwes, 2015, 2017), while other studies did not (Bucker & Theeuwes, 2014; Experiment 6 in Failing & Theeuwes, 2017). Although the reward-driven attentional bias occurred in all of these experiments, other experiments suggest that, at least in non-sparse displays, some degree of initial attentional prioritization through means of task relevance, physical salience or explicit knowledge about the stimulus-reward relationship may be beneficial, if not necessary, to develop a reward-driven attentional bias (Failing & Theeuwes, 2017). However, how exactly these factors influence the development of the reward-based selection history bias is still unknown. In any case, this highlights the importance of addressing potential interactions between bottom-up, top-down and (reward-based) selection history processes in future studies.

More recently, Le Pelley and colleagues also provided evidence that Pavlovian association determines reward-driven biases in temporal attention (Le Pelley et al., 2017; Le Pelley et al., 2018). In one study, they made use of the AB task in which observers were required to identify the rotation direction of a single, rotated picture embedded in a stream of briefly presented non-rotated pictures (Le Pelley et al., 2017). One of the non-rotated pictures, which was

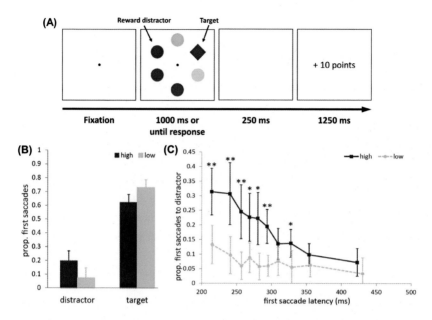

Figure 6 Trial sequence and results of Failing et al. (2015). **(A)** Observers had to make a speeded saccade to the shape singleton while ignoring all color information. Crucially, the presence of a non-salient, nontarget element in a certain color, the reward distractor, indicated how much reward could be earned for a correct and quick response (e.g., red ≙ high reward, green ≙ low reward). **(B)** Proportion of first saccades to the distractor and the target: significantly more first saccades went toward the distractor signaling a high reward. **(C)** Proportion of first saccades to the distractor and the target as a function of saccade latency: particularly the fastest first saccades are directed toward the high reward distractor (figure adapted from Failing et al., 2015).

shown for either a short or a long interval prior to the target picture, was associated with either winning or losing a reward. Observers performed worse when a picture signaling a reward was present prior to the target relative to when no reward was signaled or the reward-associated picture was absent. Note that since this study did not have a separate training phase in which the pictures were associated with reward, these reward-associated distractor pictures had been task irrelevant throughout the entire experiment and their reward biases thus came about simply by their reward-signaling value. Moreover, this effect was observed with and without explicit knowledge about the stimulus-reward association, and also when observers were explicitly informed that attending to the picture would most likely lead to a reduction in reward payout. This demonstrates that stimuli that were always completely irrelevant to the task at hand

interfered with temporal attention even when observers knew and/or experienced that this was detrimental to obtaining reward.

In short, associating reward with a salient but entirely task-irrelevant stimulus
can modulate the amount of capture elicited by that stimulus irrespective of the
consequences that it has on obtaining the reward (Le Pelley et al., 2015; Pearson
et al., 2015). Yet, while originally only shown with physically salient stimuli,
this effect also extends to stimuli that are not only never task relevant but also
never physically salient (Bucker & Theeuwes, 2017; Failing et al., 2015; Failing
& Theeuwes, 2017; Le Pelley et al., 2017). Together, this suggests that
Pavlovian associations drive reward-driven biases in spatial as well as temporal
attentional selection. While this is not to say that all attentional biases due to
reward are due to Pavlovian associations, the question as to whether Pavlovian
and instrumental associations may or may not act independently remains.

4.3 Statistical Regularities

Until now, we have discussed the evidence for two ways in which information
selected in the past will affect the way we select information in the future.
Intertrial priming as discussed earlier is an example of a short-term effect of how
the selection taking place in the previous trial (or few trials) affects selection in
the current trials. Yet, at a more general level, it is known that observers learn
about the structure and regularities present in the environment, which in turn
may also affect attentional selection. Extracting regularities from the environment in service of automatic behavior is one of the most fundamental abilities of
any living organism and is often referred to as statistical learning. It is assumed
to be a largely unconscious, unintentional and thus an implicit cognitive process
(e.g., Turk-Browne, Jungé & Scholl, 2005). Statistical learning may not only
play a role in attentional selection but is also a much more fundamental ability
that plays a crucial role in the acquisition of many skills such as language, motor
skills and object recognition. For example, one of the most well-known findings in the statistical learning literature is that infants exposed to nonsense
streams of speech for two minutes only react differently to hearing "pseudo-
words" as opposed to "nonwords." This indicates that infants learn which syllabi
are always paired together (Saffran, Aslin & Newport, 1996).

Classic research has furthermore shown that human observers also implicitly
learn auditory and/or visual patterns that are defined probabilistically. For
example, several studies investigating visual statistical learning (VSL) have
demonstrated that observers can learn relationships among visual objects.
Following the classic work on syllable learning (Saffran et al., 1996), several
studies used sequentially presented shapes in which subtle relationships were

introduced (Fiser & Aslin, 2002a, 2002b; Turk-Browne et al., 2005; Zhao, Al-Aidroos & Turk-Browne, 2013). In Fiser and Aslin (2002a), observers were exposed to a continuous stream of nonsense shapes, in which particular triplets (three shapes presented in a sequence) could appear. Later, during a surprise recall task, observers indicated a greater familiarity with the triplets than with triplets of shapes that were never presented together (so-called foil triplets), indicating that they learned higher transitional probabilities between the shapes. Because statistical learning was observed when stimuli were viewed passively without any explicit task (Fiser & Aslin, 2001) and when observers were performing a completely different and unrelated task (Saffran, Newport, Aslin, Tunick & Barrueco, 1997), it was argued that the mere exposure to these streams was enough to learn these regularities (e.g., Fiser & Aslin, 2002a). Subsequent studies, however, showed that without visual attention devoted to the stream of stimuli, no learning occurred (Turk-Browne et al., 2005) – although this notion has been questioned in more recent studies (Musz, Weber & Thompson-Schill, 2015).

4.3.1 Contextual Regularities

Previous research has demonstrated that contextual regularities can bias attentional selection. A classic example of this research is known as "contextual cueing," which has demonstrated that search for a target is facilitated when it appears in a visual layout that was previously searched relative to visual layouts that were never seen before (Chun & Jiang, 1998, 1999; Jiang & Chun, 2001; for a review, see Goujon, Didierjean & Thorpe, 2015). In the original paradigm, observers were instructed to search for a "T" target among "L" distractors in sparsely scattered configurations. Half of the display configurations were repeated across blocks while others were only seen once (see Figure 7). The basic finding was that observers were faster in finding targets when they appeared in repeated configurations, suggesting that observers learned the association between the spatial configuration and the target location. Moreover, observers could not report which configurations they had seen before, suggesting little awareness of what they had learned (Chun & Jiang, 2003). Contextual cueing studies hence reveal that the visual system is sensitive to regularities in the environment, and that it will encode and retrieve information that is relevant for the task.

4.3.2 Temporal Regularities

Observers not only learn about the spatial configurations of a target embedded in nontargets but they also learn about temporal relationships between objects

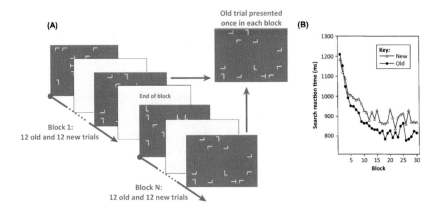

Figure 7 A typical contextual cueing task of Chun and Jiang (1998) and its findings. **(A)** Observers search for a rotated T-target among L-distractors. During each block of trials, observers search through displays having new configurations and configurations they have searched before (old). For these old configurations the target appears at consistent locations. **(B)** Typical learning pattern: over blocks of trials, observers continuously improve performance but, crucially, performance is much better for previously searched displays than for new displays (figure from Goujon et al., 2015).

(Fiser & Aslin, 2002a; Turk-Browne et al., 2005). Experiments that demonstrated statistical learning of temporal regularities were closely modeled after the original auditory statistical learning experiments. The basic paradigm involves the presentation of nonsense shapes, one after the other, as the only object on the screen. Particular shapes are presented with particular probabilities in temporal pairs or triplets. Figure 8 (the middle stream) provides an example of stimuli used by Turk-Browne and colleagues (2005) in which observers had to attend only to the green shapes while these were interleaved with red non-attended shapes. The task of the observer was to determine whether there was a repetition of the shape (1-back task). Turk-Brown and colleagues (2005) showed that observers only learned the temporal structure of the attended triplets (here green) and not of the unattended triplets (here red), providing evidence that attention in VSL is needed for learning to occur. However, the notion that attention is generally needed for learning to occur is still debated (e.g., Musz et al., 2015).

   In another study, Zhao and colleagues (2013) investigated whether temporal statistical learning influenced spatial attention. In this task, observers viewed four streams of different abstract shapes presented one after another at four different locations. These streams were occasionally interrupted by the presentation of a visual search display that contained a target and three distractors in the four stream locations. Importantly, while three streams

Attend to green (selective 1-back task)

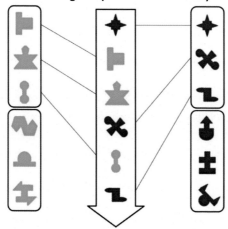

Figure 8 Example of temporal visual statistical learning. The middle stream consisting of red and green nonsense shapes is presented one shape after the other in the center of the screen. Particular shapes come in triplets. Observers only attend to one color (say, green) and have to decide whether a shape is repeated or not (1-back task). Observers learn the triplets in the attended-to color only, suggesting that attention is needed for VSL to occur (adapted from Turk-Browne et al., 2005).

showed the abstract shapes in random order, one stream had specific temporal regularities by presenting the abstract shapes in triplets. Observers responded faster and more accurately when the target happened to be at the stream location that contained temporal regularities relative to when it appeared at the location of a random stream. Critically, observers were not aware of the temporal regularities even though their attention was biased toward the location that contained the regularities. Zhao and colleagues suggested a so-called closed loop of learning. The idea is that the initial attentional focus is so broad that a bit of each stream is learned. Once the statistical regularity is sufficiently learned, attention is automatically drawn toward the spatial location containing the regular information. This bias, in turn, prioritizes the spatial location for subsequent episodes of selection, effectively reinforcing the learning process.

4.3.3 Spatial Regularities

Contextual cueing research has shown that observers are faster in finding targets when they appeared in repeated configurations, indicating that some learning of the relationship between the spatial configuration and the target location takes place. In general, these findings are consistent with the classic cueing studies by Posner (e.g., Posner, 1980), which have shown that observers are faster to detect targets appearing in probable locations than improbable locations (Shaw & Shaw, 1977). Notably, however, unlike classic cueing studies, in contextual cueing the effect occurs without instruction, without the intention or knowledge to learn. Even though it has been generally assumed that "statistical learning is constrained by top-down selective attention, i.e., that statistical learning only occurs for task-relevant objects" (Turk-Browne, 2012, p. 128, lines 16–18), recent studies indicated that observers also learn statistical regularities that are task irrelevant (e.g., Failing, Feldmann-Wüstefeld, Wang, Olivers & 2019a; Failing, Wang & Theeuwes, 2019b; Ferrante et al., 2018; Goschy, Bakos, Müller & Zehetleitner, 2014; Wang & Theeuwes, 2018a, 2018b, 2018c). These studies used a modified version of the additional singleton task in which the distractor appeared much more often in one location than in all other locations. Figure 9 presents the basic findings. The middle panel shows that a distractor singleton that appears at the more frequent location interferes much less with search for the target than when the same distractor singleton appears in another location. Attentional capture for a color distractor appearing at the high-probability (more likely) location was significantly less than when it appeared at a low-probability (less likely) location. As can be seen in the middle

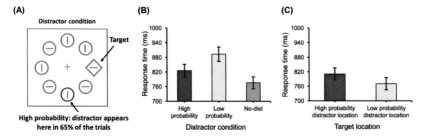

Figure 9 Example display and results. **(A)** Additional singleton paradigm. The red distractor could appear anywhere in the visual field but appeared more often in one location (high-probability location) than in all other locations (low-probability location). In one-third of the trials, the red distractor was absent (no distractor condition). **(B)** There was less attentional capture when the distractor appeared at the high-probability location than when it appeared at the low-probability location. When there was no distractor (no-dist.), observers were the fastest. **(C)** If the target happened to be presented at the high-probability distractor location in distractor-absent trials, observers were slower to select the target than when it appeared at any of the other (low-probability distractor) locations (adapted from Wang & Theeuwes, 2018b).

panel of Figure 9, relative to the no-distractor condition (blue bar), capture by a distractor at a high-probability location (red bar) is less than when a distractor appears at the low probability location (pink bar). Importantly, the right panel shows that when the target singleton happens to be presented (at chance level) at that high-probability distractor location in distractor absent trials, its selection is less efficient, as reflected by longer RT. Additionally, there was also a gradient of suppression around the high-probability location such that the further the distractor or the target was away from the high-probability distractor location, the weaker the observed effect (not shown here).

Moreover, many studies also tested whether observers were aware of the regularities. For example, in Wang and Theeuwes (2018a) observers had to indicate with a mouse click where they thought the distractor was presented most often. Most observers indicated one of the low-probability locations, suggesting that they were completely unaware of the spatial regularity. Crucially, whether observers were aware of the location had no bearing on whether or to what extent they exhibited the effect. On the basis of these findings (reduced capture, less efficient target selection and a spatial gradient), it was concluded that statistical regularities bias attention implicitly. This bias is characterized by spatial suppression of the high-probability distractor location, suggesting that this location is suppressed relative to all other locations on the attentional priority map.

Other studies have shown that observers not only suppress the location that is likely to contain a distractor but also learn to prioritize the location that is likely to contain a target (Ferrante et al., 2018; Geng & Behrmann, 2002, 2005). These studies support the view that statistical regularities bias attention either by increasing weights for locations that are relevant or by decreasing weights for locations that are irrelevant, demonstrating that selection is highly flexible and optimally adapted to the statistics of the environment.

VSL does not only affect covert attention but also affects overt attentional selection. Adapting the oculomotor capture paradigm. Wang, Samara and Theeuwes (2019) found that the distractor captures the eyes in 38 percent of the trials when presented at one of the low-probability distractor locations. However, when the distractor was presented at the high-probability distractor location, observers made far fewer errors: in only 15 percent of the trials, observers made an erroneous eye movement to the salient distractor. These findings lend further support to the conclusion that observers have started to suppress the location that is likely to contain the target as a consequence of VSL, such that this location competes less for attention than all other locations within the priority map.

Note that these results cannot be explained by some form of repetition priming or a long-level habituation process. According to the notion of repetition priming, the suppression on a previous trial determines the suppression on the current trial. However, when Wang and Theeuwes (2018b) separated trials in which the distractor appeared at the high-probability location twice in a row from trials in which it did not, the amount of suppression remained the same (see also Failing et al., 2019a; Failing et al., 2019b; Wang & Theeuwes, 2018a). Also, spatial suppression due to VSL is not a specific form of habituation. According to this notion, capture would have to be attenuated for the high-probability location because of a habituation of the capture response. Wang and Theeuwes (2018c) compared responses to a frequently occurring color distractor (e.g., a distractor with the color red) to a rarely occurring color distractor (a green distractor). If suppression would simply be habituation, one would expect that suppression of the frequently occurring color would be larger than suppression of the rare color due to dishabituation. However, no difference was found in capture between these conditions (Wang & Theeuwes, 2018b).

The research regarding statistical learning of the location of the distractor suggests that observers can learn to suppress the location of a distractor, resulting in less capture by a distractor singleton and less efficient target selection for that location. As discussed earlier, it is highly controversial whether attentional suppression is possible in a true top-down way. If anything, the results are mixed in this respect. However, the recent research concerning VSL of spatial regularities is in fact quite robust. It has been argued that through learning about regularities, specific locations within the spatial priority map may become suppressed (e.g., Failing et al., 2019a, 2019b, Failing & Theeuwes, 2020; Ferrante et al., 2018; Wang & Theeuwes, 2018a, 2018b, 2018c). The underlying mechanism has been referred to as *proactive* suppression (Chelazzi, Marini, Pascucci & Turatto, 2019; Cosman, Lowe, Zinke, Woodman & Schall, 2018; Wang, Van Driel, Ort & Theeuwes, 2019; Won, Kosoyan & Geng, 2019). In the case of VSL about spatial regularities, this refers to suppression of a location that occurs already prior to display onset. Supporting evidence for this claim comes from Wang, Van Driel and colleagues (2019), who demonstrated enhanced alpha power contralateral to the high-probability location prior to display onset. Enhanced alpha power is assumed to represent neural inhibition (Jensen & Mazaheri, 2010) and thus might serve as a general attentional gating mechanism. Moreover, Wang and colleagues (2019) showed several markers of suppression for the high-probability location in the ERP signal, notably an early P_D (74–114 ms post stimulus) and a regular P_D (186–226 ms post stimulus). They concluded that this proactive suppression is spatial in origin and basically feature blind (see also Failing et al., 2019b). Critically, this proactive suppression occurred irrespective of what is presented at that location (whether it is a target singleton or a distractor singleton).

In addition to proactive suppression induced by statistical learning, there is also what has been labeled as *reactive* suppression. This type of suppression is reactive in the sense that attention is first captured by the salient distractor (even for the briefest moment) and is then immediately suppressed (Won et al., 2019). Depending on the task, it may be possible that the disengagement of attention can be so fast that there is very little or virtually no influence of the presence of the salient distractor on selection. In other words, the presence of the distractor does not significantly slow the response to the target as disengagement from the distractor is highly efficient. This notion is similar to Moher and Egeth's (2012) conception of the "search and destroy" hypothesis. To reiterate, Moher and Egeth (2012) showed that observers who were instructed to inhibit a particular feature, could only do so after attending to the location of the to-be-ignored feature. Recent evidence suggests that these mechanisms, proactive and reactive suppression, may work in tandem to tune suppression to task-specific needs. For example, Wang and colleagues (2019) found not only reduced oculomotor capture for distractors appearing in the high-probability distractor location but also faster disengagement of attention from this location. This may suggest that in the rare event in which proactive spatial suppression fails, reactive suppression is further aiding distractor suppression. Consistent with the reactive suppression account, EEG studies found that a salient distractor first elicits an N2pc (representing a shift of attention), which is then followed by a P_D, representing its suppression (see Feldmann-Wüstefeld & Schubö 2016; Feldmann-Wüstefeld, Uengoer & Schubö 2015; Kiss, Grubert, Petersen & Eimer, 2012).

Failing and colleagues (2019b) also found evidence for proactive and reactive suppression in the same experiment. In their experiment, there were two high probability distractor locations but one of two specific distractors was more likely to appear at either of these locations. For example, while a red distractor was more probable at the top location, a green distractor was more probable at the bottom location. Consistent with proactive suppression, they found that both high-probability locations were suppressed such that target selection was impaired and interference by the distractor was reduced for these locations. Importantly though, distractor interference was even further reduced when the distractor appeared at the high-probability location at which it was highly likely to appear (e.g., the red distractor on the high-probability distractor location for red) compared to when it appeared at the high-probability location at which it was not likely to appear (e.g., the red distractor on the high-probability distractor location for green). This shows that reactive suppression further modulates the selection response and suggests that this can be a consequence of feature-specific processing on the rare occasion when attention happens to be captured by the distractor singleton.

5 Integrating Selection: The Priority Map

Based on the evidence discussed earlier in this Element, we argue that at any moment in time, three different factors – top-down, bottom-up and selection history–driven processes – determine the weights within the spatial priority map. Within this map, their respective weights are combined into a single topographic representation of the environment that determines the selection priority (e.g., which location is selected first, second, third, etc.). As noted, individual priority signals acting on this integrated priority map originate from sensory input (bottom-up), current goal states (top-down, or behavioral relevance) and statistical learning (selection history). At any given time, these signals compete with one another. In general, the notion of the priority map represents a winner-take-all neural mechanism that guides the allocation of covert and overt attention (Fecteau & Munoz, 2006; Itti & Koch, 2001; Zelinsky & Bisley, 2015). Note that it is not clear at this point how the three different factors (top-down, bottom-up and selection history–driven) interact. It is assumed that they ultimately act all on the same spatial priority map; yet it is quite feasible that, for example, spatial top-down attention and attentional biases due to statistical learning affect the control of attention independently (for a similar argument, see Jiang, 2018).

5.1 Biased Competition

In the context of a very influential neuronal model, the biased competition model, competition for neural representation is a fundamental intrinsic property of the brain and attentional selection can be understood as the process that resolves this competition (e.g., Desimone & Duncan, 1995). Within this framework, it is also assumed that early competition is dominated by the physical salience of a given stimulus, suppressing neuronal activity of other, less salient stimuli (see also the normalization model of attention, Reynolds & Heeger, 2009). Later in time, top-down control may bias the competition, for example by prioritizing a spatial location (Moran & Desimone, 1985) or the perceptual feature(s) summarized in an "attentional template" (Chelazzi, Duncan, Miller & Desimone, 1998; Reynolds, Chelazzi & Desimone, 1999). For many years, the basic conception was that only top-down and bottom-up effects operate on an integrated priority map of spatial attention. Yet, as outlined here, the new view is that in addition to top-down and bottom-up effects, previous selection experiences (i.e., selection history) also play a major role in attentional selection (Awh et al., 2012; Failing & Theeuwes, 2018; Theeuwes, 2018). Given these insights, we argue that selection history generates a priority signal that is integrated with the other signals within the integrated priority map. The activity within this map determines in an all-or-none fashion which stimulus is prioritized at any given time. Changes in the neuronal representation of a stimulus location or stimulus feature(s) due to selection history are reflected in changes within the integrated priority map.

Some researchers have argued that the priority signal due to selection history has properties that are similar to salience-induced bottom-up signals (Failing & Theeuwes, 2018, 2020; Theeuwes, 2018). Indeed, even though selection history effects have often been classified as being top-down in origin (Theeuwes, 2015, 2018), many defining characteristics of selection due to previous selection experiences are, if anything, very similar to bottom-up selection. For example, while volitional top-down selection on a given trial is typically relatively slow, history-based selection, much like bottom-up selection, is fast. Fast history–based selection has been shown in studies using reward (e.g., Anderson et al., 2011), priming (e.g., Theeuwes & Van der Burg, 2013) and learning about spatial regularities of distractors (e.g., Wang & Theeuwes, in press, 2020). Moreover, eye movement studies have clearly demonstrated a dissociation between fast history–based saccades and relatively slow, top-down saccades (Failing et al., 2015; Nissens, Failing & Theeuwes, 2016; Pearson et al., 2016; Theeuwes, 2013; Wang et al., 2019). In terms of automatic versus controlled processes as defined by Shiffrin and Schneider (1977), top-down selection is a more controlled process involving active directing, shifting and disengagement of the attentional spotlight "at will" through space (see also Posner, 1978, 1980). Yet history-based selection is basically automatic, which is exemplified by the finding that observers often fail to voluntarily counteract history-based effects. This is similar to how bottom-up attentional capture by salient single-tons typically escapes top-down control (e.g., Theeuwes, 1991a, 1992; Theeuwes et al., 2006). For example, studies in which a stimulus acquired value after it was associated with reward during a training phase show that such a stimulus captures attention as a distractor even when observers try to select the target in a reward-free test session (e.g., Anderson et al., 2011; Failing & Theeuwes, 2014) and even when they are fully aware that capture leads to worse performance and less reward payout (e.g., Failing et al., 2015; Le Pelley et al., 2015). The persistent capture by the stimulus previously associated with reward implies that the implemented top-down set cannot overcome the distraction by that stimulus. It is perhaps unsurprising, then, that some have referred to this type of selection as "habitual attention" (e.g., Anderson, 2016; Jiang, 2018). Analogous observations have been made in the context of intertrial priming of distractors irrespective of whether they were associated with reward (Hickey et al., 2010; Theeuwes, 2013). Finally, as alluded to earlier, top-down selection requires effort. Take for example a Posner cueing task in which a verbal cue points to the likely location of the target. If observers do not actively use and interpret this cue to direct their attention, no top-down cueing effect will be observed. Contrary to this, history-based selection occurs without any effort on the part of the observer. In fact, effects of history-based selection occur without observers even being aware of stimulus-reward associations (e.g., Anderson, 2015; Pearson et al., 2015; Le Pelley et al., 2015), stimulus-punishment or stimulus-threat associations (e.g., Nissens et al., 2016), simple stimulus repetitions such as in intertrial priming (Kristjánsson & Campana, 2010), or more complex statistical regularities in the display (e.g., Ferrante et al., 2018; Wang & Theeuwes, 2018a, 2018b, 2018c; Zhao et al., 2013). In other words, history-based selection often implicitly affects selection, much like physically salient objects can capture attention in a bottom-up way without the observer being aware of it (e.g., Zhang, Zhaoping, Zhou, & Fang, 2012; Zhaoping, 2008). In short, the characteristics of history-based selection are similar to those of bottom-up selection. They are fast, automatic, effortless and occur when observers are unaware of their existence or even when they attempt to counteract them in a top-down way.

5.2 Neural Mechanisms

The scientific evidence so far strongly suggests that stimuli imbued with selection history gain a competitive advantage biasing attentional selection in their favor. In this sense, it appears as if selection history creates "subjective saliency," rendering – even physically non-salient – stimuli more pertinent to the visual system. This notion is akin to what Berridge and Robinson referred to as "incentive salience" (e.g., Berridge, 2007; Berridge & Robinson, 1998) in the context of research on addiction. According to the incentive salience hypothesis, incentive salience consists of the two psychological processes of "wanting" and "liking" that become associated with a stimulus that reliably predicts reward. In essence, these processes foster the transformation of an otherwise neutral or intrinsically insignificant stimulus into a stimulus that grabs attention because it signals a desired outcome. This process is reminiscent of a facilitatory priming mechanism that, for example, when driven by reward, renders a reward-associated stimulus more salient to the visual system.

The idea that a basically neutral stimulus can gain subjective saliency, making it stand out from all other elements, implies that learning of regularities changes the representation of an object within the spatial priority map. This conception lends some evidence from classic neuroscientific studies. Bichot and Schall (2002), for example, measured the responses of individual neurons in the frontal eye fields (FEF) and showed that intertrial priming of a target stimulus changes the neural responses to target stimulus within this brain region. Since the FEF are considered to be a neural substrate of a map representing selection priority (Thompson & Bichot, 2005), this finding may be considered diagnostic of the influence of selection history on attentional selection. However, since the neuronal response modulations were observed in response to a recurring target stimulus, it is difficult to assess whether they were not simply reflecting top-down processes. In another study, Olivers and Hickey (2010) showed that intertrial priming results in latency shifts and amplitude differences in the P1 component, suggesting that some of the changes may already occur in the first feedforward sweep of information (see also, e.g., Hickey et al., 2010; MacLean & Giesbrecht, 2015). Hence, one might postulate that experience from recurrent selection of a stimulus boosts the stimulus representation above and beyond its physical salience. This notion is also in line with, for example, results from Theeuwes and Van der Burg (2013), who demonstrated that repetition priming makes an object stand out to the extent that it receives prior entry into the visual system. Similarly, Hickey and Peelen (2015, 2017) showed that representations of objects previously associated with reward are suppressed in the objective-selective cortex, which is consistent with the idea that associating the object with reward boosted its neuronal representation to the extent that it had to be suppressed to prevent it from attracting attention (for complementary findings of basic visual features in V1–V3, see Itthipuripat, Võ, Sprague & Serences, 2019). Similar observations have also been made in the context of EEG studies where stimuli or their corresponding locations that were associated with reward, primed or exhibited spatial regularities elicited a larger P_D (e.g., Hickey et al., 2010; Qi et al., 2013; Wang et al., 2019).

Although a consensus seems to emerge in the literature that attentional suppression can be the consequence of selection history (e.g., the recurrent suppression of a distractor), there is no consensus regarding the underlying mechanism yet (see, e.g., Chelazzi et al., 2019; Noonan, Crittenden, Jensen & Stokes, 2018). We would argue that as much as recurrent selection boosts a stimulus representation, recurrent suppression of a particular stimulus may in turn decrease its representation toward, or possibly even below, baseline levels (see, e.g., Feldmann-Wüstefeld & Schubö, 2016). While conclusive evidence for this or any other proposed mechanism is still lacking, at least one recent study suggests that proactive alpha suppression may allow for such a mechanism under some circumstances (Wang et al., 2019; but see Noonan et al., 2016; Van Moorselaar & Slagter, 2019).

As a consequence of changes in its representation due to selection history, a stimulus may compete more or less for attentional selection. One possibility of how these representational changes might occur in the brain is through a broad increase or decrease of firing rates in neurons specifically responding to stimuli (i.e., the visual features or feature combinations) that carry selection history. However, the repeated processing of a stimulus may (also or instead) result in cortical "sharpening" of the response (for a conceptually similar argument, see Desimone, 1996). According to this idea, there are little gain modulations in the stimulus-specific neurons. Instead, the tuning curves of these neurons become more selective (i.e., their tuning functions become narrower) to the stimulus-defining properties as a consequence of past experience. Yet to this date, it is unclear which of the two (or possibly both) mechanisms underlies selection history effects.

In addition to the ongoing scientific discourse of how selection history effects might be represented and functionally integrated in the brain, the origin of their selection signals and via which pathways they map onto the priority map are not immediately clear. It appears that instead of a single brain area, these signals emerge from an entire network of brain regions. Figure 10 shows an overview of

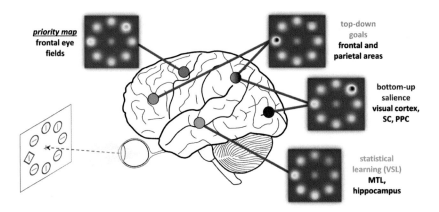

Figure 10 Simplified overview of the different factors and presumed brain regions involved in attentional selection. The priority map emerges from a distributed network involving frontal, partial, temporal areas. It is assumed that frontal brain areas (including anterior cingulate) are concerned with the top-down goals; early visual areas and structures like the superior colliculus (Itti & Koch, 2001) are involved in bottom-up salience calculations, and the medial temporal lobe (including hippocampus) is involved in storing and representing selection history (or visual statistical learning). These three signals feed into the priority map (possibly within the FEF; Thompson & Bichot, 2005), which ultimately determines selection (adapted from Theeuwes, 2019).

the three factors and their candidate brain areas. It is assumed that the spatial priority map is associated with a brain network consisting of the frontal eye field (FEF; Thompson et al., 1996), lateral parietal area (LIP; Bisley & Goldberg, 2010; Thomas & Paré, 2007) superior colliculus (SC, Fecteau & Munoz, 2006; White et al., 2017), area V1 (Li, 2002) and the caudate nucleus in the basal ganglia (Hikosaka et al., ; Hikosaka et al., 2000).

One core assumption of many salience models is that bottom-up salience calculations take place across the entire visual field for the various feature channels using different spatial scales (e.g., Itti & Koch, 2001). Yet it is unlikely that a single brain area functions as a saliency map. Instead, many brain areas – most likely operating collectively – represent the saliency map, including, for example, the FEF (Schall & Hanes, 1993), LIP (Bisley & Goldberg, 2010), SC (McPeek & Keller, 2002) and substantia nigra (Basso & Wurtz, 1997). This suggests that while salience calculations do in fact occur, it is not immediately clear whether there is a "master" saliency map. On the other hand, where top-down attention is coming from is far less clear. Top-down signals are generally assumed to derive from frontal and parietal areas (Baluch & Itti, 2011; Peelen, Heslenfeld & Theeuwes, 2004) and propagate (downstream) along the visual hierarchy through massive recurrent feedback processing (e.g., Lamme & Roelfsema, 2000). Yet, compared to the brain areas believed to code for bottom-up saliency, the specific contributions of the brain areas involved in top-down attention are largely still a matter of debate (Katsuki & Constantinidis, 2014).

As selection is predominantly spatial in origin, finding multiple topographic-ally organized maps across the entire brain may be the consequence of coding in a common (spatial) reference frame that presumably reduces overhead process-ing. Additionally, while it may be that each map represents predominantly signals of a specific process, signals of other processes may also be represented in other maps depending on the task, context or time in which selection takes place. Indeed, due to constantly ongoing feedforward and feedback information it is difficult to isolate individual processes. This is particularly problematic when moment-to-moment fluctuations in these processes cannot always be measured accurately, as it is often the case for top-down processes.

A conception that has gained traction over the years is that what appears to be allowing the communication within this network of brain areas are neuronal oscillations (e.g., Fries, 2005; Jensen, Gips, Bergmann & Bonnefond, 2014; Popov, Kastner & Jensen, 2017). Particularly alpha oscillations have been identified as instrumental in directing the network to selectively prioritize information for attention. However, it remains unclear whether the role of alpha oscillations lies more in the enhancement of relevant or the suppression of irrelevant stimuli (cf. Foster & Awh, 2018; Foxe & Snyder, 2011; Slagter, Prinssen, Reteig & Mazaheri, 2016).

In order to extract information and form a representation of the environment, configurations of multiple visual stimuli have to be bound together. When speculating about the neural mechanisms involved in selection due to learning experience (statistical learning), the hippocampal system (hippocampus and associated medial temporal lobe structures; MTL) is therefore a likely candidate (e.g., Gaffan, 1994; Holland & Bouton, 1999; Murray & Mishkin, 1998; Schapiro, Turk-Browne, Norman & Botvinick, 2016; but see Rungratsameetaweemana, Squire & Serences, 2019). Research has shown that some neurons in the hippocampal system have tuning properties optimized to respond to recurring features in the visual input (Staresina & Davachi, 2009; Wallenstein, Hasselmo & Eichenbaum, 1998). The hippocampus has also been shown to be well suited to extract regularities from the environment, including the memorization of specific contexts in which these regularities were extracted. An fMRI study by Shapiro and colleagues (1997), for example, found that changes in the hippocampus reflected the learning of temporal relationships between pairs of objects. This occurred even though observers were not instructed to attend to these regularities. Observers also had no conscious access to these memories, which suggests a major role for the hippocampus in implicit learning as well. Complementary evidence comes from lesion studies showing severely impaired learning of contextual regularities in patients with damage in the hippocampus/MTL (Eichenbaum, Yonelinas & Ranganath, 2007). For instance, Chun and Phelps (1999) showed that while patients with damage in the hippocampus exhibited normal skills learning, they did not show contextual cueing effects (see also Spaak & Lange, 2020).

Although it appears that the hippocampus and the MTL may be important for selection history effects, note that typically no involvement of the hippocampus is found in perceptual priming. Instead, perceptual priming has often been linked to modulations occurring directly in the sensory cortical areas involved in the initial perception (e.g., Schacter & Buckner, 1998; Squire & Zola, 1996). However, the absence of hippocampal involvement in priming may hint toward a potential distinction in the mechanism underlying the influence of selection history. It is conceivable that this distinction corresponds to selection history being driven either by simple memory types (e.g., habituation and sensitization) or by the extraction of more complex relationships (Batterink, Paller & Reber, 2019). On the one hand, effects based on simple memory types, such as perceptual priming (and by extension intertrial or repetition priming), may thus only recruit the neural circuits that were active during initial perception and learning. On the other hand, the hippocampus and MTL might be (additionally) involved when more complex regularities are extracted. In fact, this distinction at the neuronal level would correspond well with behavioral findings. Indeed, the effect of contextual, spatial or temporal regularities on selection is oftentimes considerably larger than the effect of intertrial priming.

6 Conclusions

The present Element presents a new framework in which attentional control is the result of the interaction between top-down, bottom-up and selection history effects. We argue that the role of top-down volitional control is rather limited; instead attentional selection is more often than previously assumed the result of lingering biases of previous selection episodes. We argue that the properties of history-based selection biases are very similar to bottom-up effects on attention. The history-based lingering biases occur relatively fast, are automatic and effortless and take place when observers are unaware of them or even when they try to counteract them in a top-down way. We furthermore argue that history-based attentional prioritization is achieved through changes in the neuronal representation of a stimulus. This representation changes because of the learned experiences with previous episodes of selecting this particular stimulus and/or location. The effect of learning is that it may make the stimulus and/or its location either more prominent (enhancement) or less prominent (suppression) biasing attentional selection.

References

Anderson, B. A. (2013). A value-driven mechanism of attentional selection. *Journal of Vision*, *13*(3), 1–17.

Anderson, B. A. (2016a). The attention habit: How reward learning shapes attentional selection. *Annals of the New York Academy of Sciences*, *1369*(1), 24–39.

Anderson, B. A. (2016b). Value-driven attentional capture in the auditory domain. *Attention, Perception, & Psychophysics*, *78*(1), 242–250.

Anderson, B. A. & Halpern, M. (2017). On the value-dependence of value-driven attentional capture. *Attention, Perception, & Psychophysics*, *79*(4), 1001–1011.

Anderson, B. A. & Kim, H. (2019). On the relationship between value-driven and stimulus-driven attentional capture. *Attention, Perception, & Psychophysics*, *81*(3), 607–613. http://doi.org/10.3758/s13414-019-01670-2

Anderson, B. A., Kronemer, S. I., Rilee, J. J., Sacktor, N. & Marvel, C. L. (2016). Reward, attention, and HIV-related risk in HIV+ individuals. *Neurobiology of Disease*, *92*, 157–165.

Anderson, B. A., Laurent, P. A. & Yantis, S. (2011). Value-driven attentional capture. *Proceedings of the National Academy of Sciences*, *108*(25), 10367–10371.

Anderson, B. A., Laurent, P. A. & Yantis, S. (2014). Value-driven attentional priority signals in human basal ganglia and visual cortex. *Brain Research*, *1587*, 88–96.

Anderson, B. A. & Yantis, S. (2012). Value-driven attentional and oculomotor capture during goal-directed, unconstrained viewing. *Attention, Perception, & Psychophysics*, *74*(8), 1644–1653.

Ansorge, U., Kiss, M., Worschech, F. & Eimer, M. (2011). The initial stage of visual selection is controlled by top-down task set: New ERP evidence. *Attention, Perception, & Psychophysics*, *73*, 113–122.

Asutay, E. & Västfjäll, D. (2016). Auditory attentional selection is biased by reward cues. *Scientific Reports*, 36989.

Awh, E., Belopolsky, A. & Theeuwes, J. (2012). Top-down versus bottom-up attentional control: A failed theoretical dichotomy. *Trends in Cognitive Sciences*, *16*(8), 437–443.

Bacon, W. F. & Egeth, H. E. (1994). Overriding stimulus-driven attentional capture. *Perception & Psychophysics*, *55*(5), 485–496.

Baluch, F. & Itti, L. (2011). Mechanisms of top-down attention. *Trends in Neurosciences*, *34*(4), 210–224.

Barras, C. & Kerzel, D. (2016). Active suppression of salient-but-irrelevant stimuli does not underlie resistance to visual interference. *Biological Psychology, 121*, 74–83.

Basso, M. A. & Wurtz, R. H. (1997). Modulation of neuronal activity by target uncertainty. *Nature, 389*(6646), 66–69.

Batterink, L. J., Paller, K. A. & Reber, P. J. (2019). Understanding the neural bases of implicit and statistical learning. *Topics in Cognitive Science*. http://doi.org/10.1111/tops.12420

Belopolsky, A. V., Schreij, D. & Theeuwes, J. (2010). What is top-down about contingent capture? *Attention, Perception, & Psychophysics, 72*(2), 326–341.

Berridge, K. C. (2007). The debate over dopamine's role in reward: The case for incentive salience. *Psychopharmacology, 191*(3), 391–431.

Berridge, K. C. & Robinson, T. E. (1998). What is the role of dopamine in reward: Hedonic impact, reward learning, or incentive salience? *Brain Research Reviews, 28*(3), 309–369.

Berridge, K. C., Robinson, T. E. & Aldridge, J. W. (2009). Dissecting components of reward: "Liking," "wanting," and learning. *Current Opinion in Pharmacology, 9*(1), 65–73.

Bichot, N. P. & Schall, J. D. (2002). Priming in macaque frontal cortex during popout visual search: Feature-based facilitation and location-based inhibition of return. *Journal of Neuroscience, 22*(11), 4675–4685.

Biederman, I. (1972). Perceiving real-world scenes. *Science, 177*(4043), 77–80.

Biederman, I., Mezzanotte, R. J. & Rabinowitz, J. C. (1982). Scene perception: Detecting and judging objects undergoing relational violations. *Cognitive Psychology, 14*(2), 143–177.

Bisley, J. W. & Goldberg, M. E. (2010). Attention, intention, and priority in the parietal lobe. *Annual Review of Neuroscience, 33*, 1–21.

Born, S., Kerzel, D. & Theeuwes, J. (2011). Evidence for a dissociation between the control of oculomotor capture and disengagement. *Experimental Brain Research, 208*(4), 621–631.

Bravo, M. J. & Nakayama, K. (1992). The role of attention in different visual-search tasks. *Perception & Psychophysics, 51*, 465–472.

Bucker, B., Belopolsky, A. V. & Theeuwes, J. (2015). Distractors that signal reward attract the eyes. *Visual Cognition, 23*(1–2), 1–24.

Bucker, B., Silvis, J. D., Donk, M. & Theeuwes, J. (2015). Reward modulates oculomotor competition between differently valued stimuli. *Vision Research, 108*, 103–112.

Bucker, B. & Theeuwes, J. (2014). The effect of reward on orienting and reorienting in exogenous cuing. *Cognitive, Affective, & Behavioral Neuroscience, 14*(2), 635–646.

Bucker, B. & Theeuwes, J. (2017). Pavlovian reward learning underlies value driven attentional capture. *Attention, Perception, & Psychophysics*, *79*(2), 415–428.

Burra, N. & Kerzel, D. (2014). The distractor positivity (P_D) signals lowering of attentional priority: Evidence from event-related potentials and individual differences. *Psychophysiology*, *51*(7), 685–696.

Buschman, T. J. & Miller, E. K. (2007). Top-down versus bottom-up control of attention in the prefrontal and posterior parietal cortices. S*cience*, *315*(5820), 1860–1862.

Carrasco, M. (2011). Visual attention: The past 25 years. *Vision Research*, *51* (13), 1484–1525.

Chao, H.-F. (2010). Top-down attentional control for distractor locations: The benefit of precuing distractor locations on target localization and discrimination. *Journal of Experimental Psychology. Human Perception and Performance*, *36*, 303–316.

Chelazzi, L., Duncan, J., Miller, E. K. & Desimone, R. (1998). Responses of neurons in inferior temporal cortex during memory-guided visual search. *Journal of Neurophysiology*, *80*(6), 2918–2940.

Chelazzi, L., Eštočinová, J., Calletti, R., Gerfo, E. L., Sani, I., Della Libera, C. & Santandrea, E. (2014). Altering spatial priority maps via reward-based learning. *Journal of Neuroscience*, *34*(25), 8594–8604.

Chelazzi, L., Marini, F., Pascucci, D. & Turatto, M. (2019). Getting rid of visual distractors: The why, when, how and where. *Current Opinion in Psychology*, *29*, 135–147. http://doi.org/10.1016/j.copsyc.2019.02.004

Chelazzi, L., Perlato, A., Santandrea, E. & Della Libera, C. (2013). Rewards teach visual selective attention. *Vision Research*, *85*, 58–72.

Chun, M. M. & Jiang, Y. (1998). Contextual cueing: Implicit learning and memory of visual context guides spatial attention. *Cognitive Psychology*, *36*(1), 28–71.

Chun, M. M. & Jiang, Y. (1999). Top-down attentional guidance based on implicit learning of visual covariation. *Psychological Science*, *10*(4), 360–365.

Chun, M. M. & Jiang, Y. (2003). Implicit, long-term spatial contextual memory. *Journal of Experimental Psychology: Learning, Memory, and Cognition*, *29* (2), 224.

Chun, M. M. & Phelps, E. A. (1999). Memory deficits for implicit contextual information in amnesic subjects with hippocampal damage. *Nature Neuroscience*, *2*(9), 844–847.

Connor, C. E., Egeth, H. E. & Yantis, S. (2004). Visual attention: Bottom-up versus top-down. *Current Biology*, *14*(19), R850–R852.

Corbetta, M. & Shulman, G. L. (2002). Control of goal-directed and stimulus-driven attention in the brain. *Nature Reviews Neuroscience, 3*(3), 201–215.

Cosman, J. D., Lowe, K. A., Zinke, W., Woodman, G. F. & Schall, J. D. (2018). Prefrontal control of visual distraction. *Current Biology, 28*(3), 414–420.

Davoli, C. C., Suszko, J. W. & Abrams, R. A. (2007). New objects can capture attention without a unique luminance transient. *Psychonomic Bulletin & Review, 14*(2), 338–343.

Libera, C. & Chelazzi, L. (2006). Visual selective attention and the effects of monetary rewards. *Psychological Science, 17*(3), 222–227.

Della Libera, C. & Chelazzi, L. (2009). Learning to attend and to ignore is a matter of gains and losses. *Psychological Science, 20*(6), 778–784.

Della Libera, C., Perlato, A. & Chelazzi, L. (2011). Dissociable effects of reward on attentional learning: From passive associations to active monitoring. *PloS One, 6*(4), e19460.

Desimone, R. (1996). Neural mechanisms for visual memory and their role in attention. *Proceedings of the National Academy of Sciences, 93*(24), 13494–13499.

Desimone, R. & Duncan, J. (1995). Neural mechanisms of selective visual attention. *Annual Review of Neuroscience, 18*(1), 193–222.

Duncan, J. (1985). Two techniques for investigating perception without awareness. *Perception & Psychophysics, 38*(3), 296–298.

Dux, P. E. & Marois, R. (2009). The attentional blink: A review of data and theory. *Attention, Perception, & Psychophysics, 71*(8), 1683–1700.

Egeth, H. (2018). Comment on Theeuwes's characterization of visual selection. *Journal of Cognition, 1*(1).

Egeth, H. E. & Yantis, S. (1997). Visual attention: Control, representation, and time course. *Annual Review of Psychology, 48*(1), 269–297.

Eichenbaum, H., Yonelinas, A. P. & Ranganath, C. (2007). The medial temporal lobe and recognition memory. *Annual Review of Neuroscience, 30*, 123–152.

Eimer, M. & Kiss, M. (2008). Involuntary attentional capture is determined by task set: Evidence from event-related brain potentials. *Journal of Cognitive Neuroscience, 20*(8), 1423–1433.

Eriksen, B. A. & Eriksen, C. W. (1974). Effects of noise letters upon the identification of a target letter in a nonsearch task. *Perception & Psychophysics, 16*(1), 143–149.

Eriksen, C. W. & Hoffman, J. E. (1972). Temporal and spatial characteristics of selective encoding from visual displays. *Perception & Psychophysics, 12*(2), 201–204.

Failing, M., Feldmann-Wüstefeld, T., Wang, B., Olivers, C. & Theeuwes, J. (2019a). Statistical regularities induce spatial as well as feature-specific suppression. *Journal of Experimental Psychology: Human Perception and Performance, 45*(10), 1291–1303. http://doi.org/10.1037/xhp0000660

Failing, M., Nissens, T., Pearson, D., Le Pelley, M. & Theeuwes, J. (2015). Oculomotor capture by stimuli that signal the availability of reward. *Journal of Neurophysiology, 114*(4), 2316–2327.

Failing, M. F. & Theeuwes, J. (2014). Exogenous visual orienting by reward. *Journal of Vision, 14*(5), 6.

Failing, M. & Theeuwes, J. (2016). Reward alters the perception of time. *Cognition, 148*, 19–26.

Failing, M. & Theeuwes, J. (2017). Don't let it distract you: How information about the availability of reward affects attentional selection. *Attention, Perception, & Psychophysics, 79*(8), 2275–2298.

Failing, M. & Theeuwes, J. (2018). Selection history: How reward modulates selectivity of visual attention. *Psychonomic Bulletin & Review, 25*(2), 514–538.

Failing, M. & Theeuwes, J. (2020). More capture, more suppression: Distractor suppression due to statistical regularities is determined by the magnitude of attentional capture. *Psychonomic Bulletin & Review, 257*, 86–95.

Failing, M., Wang, B. & Theeuwes, J. (2019b). Spatial suppression due to statistical regularities is driven by distractor suppression not by target activation. *Attention, Perception, & Psychophysics*, 1–10.

Fecteau, J. H. & Munoz, D. P. (2006). Salience, relevance, and firing: A priority map for target selection. *Trends in Cognitive Sciences, 10*(8), 382–390.

Feldmann-Wüstefeld, T. & Schubö, A. (2016). Intertrial priming due to distractor repetition is eliminated in homogeneous contexts. *Attention, Perception, & Psychophysics, 78* (7), 1935–1947.

Feldmann-Wüstefeld, T., Uengoer, M. & Schubö, A. (2015). You see what you have learned. Evidence for an interrelation of associative learning and visual selective attention. *Psychophysiology, 52*, 1483–1497.

Fiser, J. & Aslin, R. N. (2001). Unsupervised statistical learning of higher-order spatial structures from visual scenes. *Psychological Science, 12*(6), 499–504.

Fiser, J. & Aslin, R. N. (2002a). Statistical learning of higher-order temporal structure from visual shape sequences. *Journal of Experimental Psychology: Learning, Memory, and Cognition, 28*(3), 458–467.

Fiser, J. & Aslin, R. N. (2002b). Statistical learning of new visual feature combinations by infants. *Proceedings of the National Academy of Sciences, 99*(24), 15822–15826.

Fockert, J. D., Rees, G., Frith, C. & Lavie, N. (2004). Neural correlates of attentional capture in visual search. *Journal of Cognitive Neuroscience, 16* (5), 751–759.

Folk, C. L., Remington, R. W. & Johnston, J. C. (1992). Involuntary covert orienting is contingent on attentional control settings. *Journal of Experimental Psychology: Human Perception and Performance, 18*(4), 1030–1040.

Foster, J. J. & Awh, E. (2018). The role of alpha oscillations in spatial attention: Limited evidence for a suppression account. *Current Opinion in Psychology, 29*, 34–40.

Found, A. & Müller, H. J. (1996). Searching for unknown feature targets on more than one dimension: Investigating a "dimension-weighting" account. *Perception & Psychophysics, 58*(1), 88–101.

Foxe, J. J. & Snyder, A. C. (2011). The role of alpha-band brain oscillations as a sensory suppression mechanism during selective attention. *Frontiers in Psychology, 2*, 154. http://doi.org/10.3389/fpsyg.2011.00154

Franconeri, S. L., Hollingworth, A. & Simons, D. J. (2005). Do new objects capture attention? *Psychological Science, 16*(4), 275–281.

Fries, P. (2005). A mechanism for cognitive dynamics: Neuronal communication through neuronal coherence. *Trends in Cognitive Sciences, 9*(10), 474–480.

Gaffan, D. (1994). Scene-specific memory for objects: A model of episodic memory impairment in monkeys with fornix transection. *Journal of Cognitive Neuroscience, 6*(4), 305–320.

Gaspelin, N., Leonard, C. J. & Luck, S. J. (2015). Direct evidence for active suppression of salient-but-irrelevant sensory inputs. *Psychological Science, 26*(11), 1740–1750.

Gaspelin, N. & Luck, S. J. (2018a). Combined electrophysiological and behavioral evidence for the suppression of salient distractors. *Journal of Cognitive Neuroscience, 30*(9), 1265–1280.

Gaspelin, N. & Luck, S. J. (2018b). The role of inhibition in avoiding distraction by salient stimuli. *Trends in Cognitive Sciences, 22*(1), 79–92.

Gaspelin, N. & Luck, S. J. (2018c). "'Top-down' does not mean 'voluntary.'" *Journal of Cognition, 1*(1), 25, 1–4.

Geng, J. J. & Behrmann, M. (2002). Probability cuing of target location facilitates visual search implicitly in normal participants and patients with hemispatial neglect. *Psychological Science, 13*(6), 520–525.

Geng, J. J. & Behrmann, M. (2005). Spatial probability as an attentional cue in visual search. *Perception & psychophysics, 67*(7), 1252–1268.

Godijn, R. & Theeuwes, J. (2002). Programming of endogenous and exogenous saccades: Evidence for a competitive integration model. *Journal of*

Experimental Psychology: Human Perception and Performance, *28*(5), 1039–1054.

Goschy, H., Bakos, S., Müller, H. J. & Zehetleitner, M. (2014). Probability cueing of distractor locations: Both intertrial facilitation and statistical learning mediate interference reduction. *Frontiers in Psychology*, *5*, 1195.

Goujon, A., Didierjean, A. & Thorpe, S. (2015). Investigating implicit statistical learning mechanisms through contextual cueing. *Trends in Cognitive Sciences*, *19*(9), 524–533.

Grubb, M. A. & Li, Y. (2018). Assessing the role of accuracy-based feedback in value-driven attentional capture. *Attention, Perception, & Psychophysics*, 1–7.

Hickey, C., Chelazzi, L. & Theeuwes, J. (2010). Reward changes salience in human vision via the anterior cingulate. *Journal of Neuroscience*, *30*(33), 11096–11103.

Hickey, C., Chelazzi, L. & Theeuwes, J. (2014). Reward-priming of location in visual search. *PloS one*, *9*(7), e103372.

Hickey, C., Di Lollo, V. & McDonald, J. J. (2009). Electrophysiological indices of target and distractor processing in visual search. *Journal of Cognitive Neuroscience*, *21*(4), 760–775.

Hickey, C. & Los, S. A. (2015). Reward priming of temporal preparation. *Visual Cognition*, *23*(1–2), 25–40.

Hickey, C. & Peelen, M. V. (2015). Neural mechanisms of incentive salience in naturalistic human vision. *Neuron*, *85*(3), 512–518.

Hickey, C. & Peelen, M. V. (2017). Reward selectively modulates the lingering neural representation of recently attended objects in natural scenes. *Journal of Neuroscience*, *37*(31), 7297–7304.

Hikosaka, O., Kim, H. F., Yasuda, M. & Yamamoto, S. (2014). Basal ganglia circuits for reward value-guided behavior. *Annual Review of Neuroscience*, *37*, 289–309.

Hikosaka, O., Takikawa, Y. & Kawagoe, R. (2000). Role of the basal ganglia in the control of purposive saccadic eye movements. *Physiological Reviews*, *80* (3), 953–978.

Hillstrom, A. P. (2000). Repetition effects in visual search. *Perception & Psychophysics*, *62*(4), 800–817.

Hillyard, S. A., Vogel, E. K. & Luck, S. J. (1998). Sensory gain control (amplification) as a mechanism of selective attention: Electrophysiological and neuroimaging evidence. *Philosophical Transactions of the Royal Society of London B: Biological Sciences*, *353*(1373), 1257–1270.

Holland, P. C. & Bouton, M. E. (1999). Hippocampus and context in classical conditioning. *Current Opinion in Neurobiology*, *9*(2), 195–202.

Hopfinger, J. B., Buonocore, M. H. & Mangun, G. R. (2000). The neural mechanisms of top-down attentional control. *Nature Neuroscience, 3*(3), 284–291.

Itthipuripat, S., Võ, V. A., Sprague, T. C. & Serences, J. (2019). Value-driven attentional capture enhances distractor representations in early visual cortex. *BioRxiv*, 567354.

Itti, L. & Koch, C. (2000). A saliency-based search mechanism for overt and covert shifts of visual attention. *Vision Research*, 1489–1506.

Itti, L. & Koch, C. (2001). Computational modelling of visual attention. *Nature Reviews Neuroscience, 2*(3), 194–203.

Itti, L., Koch, C. & Niebur, E. (1998). A model of saliency-based visual attention for rapid scene analysis. *IEEE Transactions on Pattern Analysis & Machine Intelligence*, (11), 1254–1259.

Jensen, O., Gips, B., Bergmann, T. O. & Bonnefond, M. (2014). Temporal coding organized by coupled alpha and gamma oscillations prioritize visual processing. *Trends in Neurosciences, 37*(7), 357–369.

Jensen, O. & Mazaheri, A. (2010). Shaping functional architecture by oscillatory alpha activity: Gating by inhibition. *Frontiers in Human Neuroscience, 4*, 186.

Jiang, Y. V. (2018). Habitual versus goal-driven attention. *Cortex, 102*, 107–120.

Jiang, Y. V. & Chun, M. M. (2001). Selective attention modulates implicit learning. *Quarterly Journal of Experimental Psychology: Section A, 54*(4), 1105–1124.

Jiang, Y. V., Li, Z. S. & Remington, R. W. (2015). Modulation of spatial attention by goals, statistical learning, and monetary reward. *Attention, Perception, & Psychophysics, 77*(7), 2189–2206.

Jonides, J. (1981). Voluntary versus automatic control over the mind's eye's movement. *Attention and Performance*, 187–203.

Jonides, J. & Yantis, S. (1988). Uniqueness of abrupt visual onset in capturing attention. *Perception & Psychophysics, 43*(4), 346–354.

Kahneman, D., Treisman, A. & Burkell, J. (1983). The cost of visual filtering. *Journal of Experimental Psychology: Human Perception and Performance, 9*(4), 510–522.

Katsuki, F. & Constantinidis, C. (2014). Bottom-up and top-down attention: Different processes and overlapping neural systems. *Neuroscientist, 20*(5), 509–521.

Kerzel, D. & Witzel, C. (2019). The allocation of resources in visual working memory and multiple attentional templates. *Journal of Experimental Psychology: Human Perception and Performance, 45*(5), 645–658.

Kim, M. S. & Cave, K. R. (1995). Spatial attention in visual search for features and feature conjunctions. *Psychological Science, 6*(6), 376–380.

Kim, H. F. & Hikosaka, O. (2013). Distinct basal ganglia circuits controlling behaviors guided by flexible and stable values. *Neuron, 79*(5), 1001–1010.

Kiss, M., Grubert, A., Petersen, A. & Eimer, M. (2012). Attentional capture by salient distractors during visual search is determined by temporal task demands. *Journal of Cognitive Neuroscience, 24*(3), 749–759.

Koch, C. & Ullman, S. (1985). Shifts in visual attention: Towards the underlying circuitry. *Human Neurobiology, 4*, 219–227.

Kristjánsson, Á. (2010). Priming in visual search: A spanner in the works for Theeuwes's bottom-up attention sweeps? *Acta Psychologica, 135*(2), 114.

Kristjánsson, Á. & Campana, G. (2010). Where perception meets memory: A review of repetition priming in visual search tasks. *Attention, Perception, & Psychophysics, 72*(1), 5–18.

Kumada, T. (1999). Limitations in attending to a feature value for overriding stimulus-driven interference. *Perception & Psychophysics, 61*, 61–79.

Lamme, V. A. & Roelfsema, P. R. (2000). The distinct modes of vision offered by feedforward and recurrent processing. *Trends in Neurosciences, 23*(11), 571–579.

Lamy, D. F. & Kristjánsson, Á. (2013). Is goal-directed attentional guidance just intertrial priming? A review. *Journal of Vision, 13*(3), 14. http://doi.org/10.1167/13.3.14

Le Pelley, M. E., Mitchell, C. J., Beesley, T., George, D. N. & Wills, A. J. (2016). Attention and associative learning in humans: An integrative review. *Psychological Bulletin, 142*(10), 1111–1140.

Le Pelley, M. E., Pearson, D., Griffiths, O. & Beesley, T. (2015). When goals conflict with values: Counterproductive attentional and oculomotor capture by reward-related stimuli. *Journal of Experimental Psychology: General, 144*(1), 158–171.

Le Pelley, M. E., Seabrooke, T., Kennedy, B. L., Pearson, D. & Most, S. B. (2017). Miss it and miss out: Counterproductive nonspatial attentional capture by task-irrelevant, value-related stimuli. *Attention, Perception, & Psychophysics*, 1–15.

Le Pelley, M. E., Watson, P., Pearson, D., Abeywickrama, R. S. & Most, S. B. (2018). Winners and losers: Reward and punishment produce biases in temporal selection. *Journal of Experimental Psychology: Learning, Memory, and Cognition, 45*(5), 822–833. http://doi.org/10.1037/xlm0000612

Leber, A. B. & Egeth, H. E. (2006). It's under control: Top-down search strategies can override attentional capture. *Psychonomic Bulletin & Review, 13*(1), 132–138.

Li, Z. (2002). A saliency map in primary visual cortex. *Trends in Cognitive Sciences, 6*(1), 9–16.

Luck, S. J. & Hillyard, S. A. (1994). Electrophysiological correlates of feature analysis during visual search. *Psychophysiology, 31*(3), 291–308.

Ludwig, C. J. & Gilchrist, I. D. (2002). Stimulus-driven and goal-driven control over visual selection. *Journal of Experimental Psychology: Human Perception and Performance, 28*(4), 902–912. http://doi.org/10.1037/0096-1523.28.4.902

MacLean, M. H. & Giesbrecht, B. (2015). Neural evidence reveals the rapid effects of reward history on selective attention. *Brain Research, 1606*, 86–94.

Maljkovic, V. & Nakayama, K. (1994). Priming of pop-out: I. Role of features. *Memory & Cognition, 22*(6), 657–672.

Maljkovic, V. & Nakayama, K. (2000). Priming of popout: III. A short-term implicit memory system beneficial for rapid target selection. *Visual Cognition, 7*(5), 571–595.

Martens, S. & Wyble, B. (2010). The attentional blink: Past, present, and future of a blind spot in perceptual awareness. *Neuroscience & Biobehavioral Reviews, 34*(6), 947–957.

McPeek, R. M. & Keller, E. L. (2002). Saccade target selection in the superior colliculus during a visual search task. *Journal of Neurophysiology, 88*(4), 2019–2034.

McPeek, R. M., Maljkovic, V. & Nakayama, K. (1999). Saccades require focal attention and are facilitated by a short-term memory system. *Vision Research, 39*(8), 1555–1566.

Mine, C. & Saiki, J. (2015). Task-irrelevant stimulus-reward association induces value-driven attentional capture. *Attention, Perception, & Psychophysics, 77*(6), 1896–1907.

Moher, J. & Egeth, H. E. (2012). The ignoring paradox: Cueing distractor features leads first to selection, then to inhibition of to-be-ignored items. *Attention, Perception, & Psychophysics, 74*(8), 1590–1605.

Moran, J. &. Desimone, R. (1985). Selective attention gates visual processing in the extrastriate cortex. *Science, 229*, 782–784.

Müller, H. J., Heller, D. & Ziegler, J. (1995). Visual search for singleton feature targets within and across feature dimensions. *Perception & Psychophysics, 57*(1), 1–17.

Müller, H. J. & Rabbitt, P. M. (1989). Reflexive and voluntary orienting of visual attention: Time course of activation and resistance to interruption. *Journal of Experimental Psychology: Human Perception and Performance, 15*(2), 315.

Munneke, J., Van der Stigchel, S. & Theeuwes, J. (2008). Cueing the location of a distractor: An inhibitory mechanism of spatial attention? *Acta Psychologica, 129*(1), 101–107.

Musz, E., Weber, M. J. & Thompson-Schill, S. L. (2015). Visual statistical learning is not reliably modulated by selective attention to isolated events. *Attention, Perception, & Psychophysics, 77*(1), 78–96.

Neumann, O. (1984). Automatic processing: A review of recent findings and a plea for an old theory. In *Cognition and motor processes* (pp. 255–293). Berlin: Springer.

Nissens, T., Failing, M. & Theeuwes, J. (2016). People look at the object they fear: oculomotor capture by stimuli that signal threat. *Cognition and Emotion, 31*, 1–8. http://doi.org/10.1080/02699931.2016.1248905

Noonan, M. P., Adamian, N., Pike, A., Printzlau, F., Crittenden, B. M. & Stokes, M. G. (2016). Distinct mechanisms for distractor suppression and target facilitation. *Journal of Neuroscience, 36*(6), 1797–1807.

Noonan, M. P., Crittenden, B. M., Jensen, O. & Stokes, M. G. (2018). Selective inhibition of distracting input. *Behavioural Brain Research, 355*, 36–47.

Olivers, C. N. & Hickey, C. (2010). Priming resolves perceptual ambiguity in visual search: Evidence from behaviour and electrophysiology. *Vision Research, 50*(14), 1362–1371.

Olivers, C. N. & Humphreys, G. W. (2003). Visual marking inhibits singleton capture. *Cognitive Psychology, 47*(1), 1–42.

Pearson, D., Donkin, C., Tran, S. C., Most, S. B. & Le Pelley, M. E. (2015). Cognitive control and counterproductive oculomotor capture by reward-related stimuli. *Visual Cognition, 23*(1–2), 41–66.

Pearson, D., Osborn, R., Whitford, T. J., Failing, M., Theeuwes, J. & Le Pelley, M. E. (2016). Value-modulated oculomotor capture by task-irrelevant stimuli is feature-specific. *Attention, Perception & Psychophysics, 78*(7), 2226–2240.

Peck, C. J., Jangraw, D. C., Suzuki, M., Efem, R. & Gottlieb, J. (2009). Reward modulates attention independently of action value in posterior parietal cortex. *Journal of Neuroscience, 29*(36), 11182–11191.

Peelen, M. V., Heslenfeld, D. J. & Theeuwes, J. (2004). Endogenous and exogenous attention shifts are mediated by the same large-scale neural network. *Neuroimage, 22*(2), 822–830.

Pinto, Y., Olivers, C. L. & Theeuwes, J. (2005). Target uncertainty does not lead to more distraction by singletons: Intertrial priming does. *Perception & Psychophysics, 67*(8), 1354–1361.

Pollmann, S., Eštočinová, J., Sommer, S., Chelazzi, L. & Zinke, W. (2016). Neural structures involved in visual search guidance by reward-enhanced contextual cueing of the target location. *Neuroimage*, *124*, 887–897.

Popov, T., Kastner, S. & Jensen, O. (2017). FEF-controlled alpha delay activity precedes stimulus-induced gamma-band activity in visual cortex. *Journal of Neuroscience*, *37*(15), 4117–4127.

Posner, M. I. (1978). *Chronometric explorations of mind.* Hillsdale, NJ: Erlbaum.

Posner, M. I. (1980). Orienting of Attention. *Quarterly Journal of Experimental Psychology*, *32*, 3–25.

Posner, M. I. & Cohen, Y. (1984). Components of visual orienting. *Attention and Performance X: Control of Language Processes*, *32*, 531–556.

Posner, M. I., Nissen, M. J. & Ogden, W. C. (1978). Attended and unattended processing modes: The role of set for spatial location. *Modes of Perceiving and Processing Information*, *137*(158), 2.

Posner, M. I., Snyder, C. R. & Davidson, B. J. (1980). Attention and the detection of signals. *Journal of Experimental Psychology: General*, *109*(2), 160.

Postle, B. R. & D'Esposito, M. (1999). Dissociation of human caudate nucleus activity in spatial and nonspatial working memory: An event-related fMRI study. *Cognitive Brain Research*, *8*(2), 107–115.

Postle, B. R. & D'Esposito, M. (2003). Spatial working memory activity of the caudate nucleus is sensitive to frame of reference. *Cognitive, Affective, & Behavioral Neuroscience*, *3*(2), 133–144.

Qi, S., Zeng, Q., Ding, C. & Li, H. (2013). Neural correlates of reward-driven attentional capture in visual search. *Brain Research*, *1532*, 32–43.

Rajsic, J., Perera, H. & Pratt, J. (2016). Learned value and object perception: Accelerated perception or biased decisions? *Attention, Perception, & Psychophysics*, 1–11.

Raymond, J. E. & O'Brien, J. L. (2009). Selective visual attention and motivation: The consequences of value learning in an attentional blink task. *Psychological Science*, *20*(8), 981–988.

Raymond, J. E., Shapiro, K. L. & Arnell, K. M. (1992). Temporary suppression of visual processing in an RSVP task: An attentional blink? *Journal of Experimental Psychology: Human Perception and Performance*, *18*(3), 849–860.

Reynolds, J. H., Chelazzi, L. & Desimone, R. (1999). Competitive mechanisms subserve attention in macaque areas V2 and V4. *Journal of Neuroscience*, *19* (5), 1736–1753.

Reynolds, J. H. & Heeger, D. J. (2009). The normalization model of attention. *Neuron, 61*(2), 168–185.

Ristic, J. & Kingstone, A. (2006). Attention to arrows: Pointing to a new direction. *Quarterly Journal of Experimental Psychology, 59*(11), 1921–1930.

Roper, Z. J., Vecera, S. P. & Vaidya, J. G. (2014). Value-driven attentional capture in adolescence. *Psychological Science, 25*(11), 1987–1993.

Ruff, C. C. & Driver, J. (2006). Attentional preparation for a lateralized visual distractor: Behavioral and fMRI evidence. *Journal of Cognitive Neuroscience, 18*(4), 522–538.

Rungratsameetaweemana, N., Squire, L. R. & Serences, J. T. (2019). Preserved capacity for learning statistical regularities and directing selective attention after hippocampal lesions. *Proceedings of the National Academy of Sciences, 116*(39), 19705–19710.

Saffran, J. R., Aslin, R. N. & Newport, E. L. (1996). Statistical learning by 8-month-old infants. *Science, 274*(5294), 1926–1928.

Saffran, J. R., Newport, E. L., Aslin, R. N., Tunick, R. A. & Barrueco, S. (1997). Incidental language learning: Listening (and learning) out of the corner of your ear. *Psychological Science, 8*(2), 101–105.

Sawaki, R. & Luck, S. J. (2010). Capture versus suppression of attention by salient singletons: Electrophysiological evidence for an automatic attend-to-me signal. *Attention, Perception, & Psychophysics, 72*(6), 1455–1470.

Sawaki, R., Geng, J. J. & Luck, S. J. (2012). A common neural mechanism for preventing and terminating attention. *Journal of Neuroscience, 32*, 10725–10736. http://doi.org/10.1523/JNEUROSCI.1864-12.2012

Schacter, D. L. & Buckner, R. L. (1998). Priming and the brain. *Neuron, 20*(2), 185–195.

Schall, J. D. & Hanes, D. P. (1993). Neural basis of saccade target selection in frontal eye field during visual search. *Nature, 366*(6454), 467–469.

Schapiro, A. C., Turk-Browne, N. B., Norman, K. A. & Botvinick, M. M. (2016). Statistical learning of temporal community structure in the hippocampus. *Hippocampus, 26*(1), 3–8.

Schoeberl, T., Goller, F. & Ansorge, U. (2019). Testing a priming account of the contingent capture effect. *Attention, Perception, & Psychophysics, 81*, 1262–1282.

Schreij, D., Owens, C. & Theeuwes, J. (2008). Abrupt onsets capture attention independent of top-down control settings. *Perception & Psychophysics, 70*(2), 208–218.

Schreij, D., Theeuwes, J. & Olivers, C. N. (2010). Abrupt onsets capture attention independent of top-down control settings II: Additivity is no evidence for filtering. *Attention, Perception, & Psychophysics, 72*(3), 672–682.

Schultz, W. (2016). Dopamine reward prediction-error signalling: A two-component response. *Nature Reviews Neuroscience, 17*(3), 183–195.

Serences, J. T. (2008). Value-based modulations in human visual cortex. *Neuron, 60*(6), 1169–1181.

Serences, J. T. & Saproo, S. (2010). Population response profiles in early visual cortex are biased in favor of more valuable stimuli. *Journal of Neurophysiology, 104*(1), 76–87.

Serences, J. T., Shomstein, S., Leber, A. B., Golay, X., Egeth, H. E. & Yantis, S. (2005). Coordination of voluntary and stimulus-driven attentional control in human cortex. *Psychological Science, 16*(2), 114–122.

Serences, J. T., Yantis, S., Culberson, A. & Awh, E. (2004). Preparatory activity in visual cortex indexes distractor suppression during covert spatial orienting. *Journal of Neurophysiology, 92*(6), 3538–3545.

Shapiro, K. L., Raymond, J. E. & Arnell, K. M. (1997). The attentional blink. *Trends in Cognitive Sciences, 1*(8),291–296.

Shaw, M. L. & Shaw, P. (1977). Optimal allocation of cognitive resources to spatial locations. Journal of Experimental Psychology. *Human Perception and Performance, 3*, 201–211.

Sheliga, B. M., Riggio, L. & Rizzolatti, G. (1994). Orienting of attention and eye movements. *Experimental Brain Research, 98*(3), 507–522.

Shiffrin, R. M. & Schneider, W. (1977). Controlled and automatic human information processing: II. Perceptual learning, automatic attending and a general theory. *Psychological Review, 84*(2), 127–190.

Sisk, C. A., Remington, R. W. & Jiang, Y. V. (2018). The risks of downplaying top-down control. *Journal of Cognition, 1*(1).

Slagter, H. A., Prinssen, S., Reteig, L. C. & Mazaheri, A. (2016). Facilitation and inhibition in attention: functional dissociation of pre-stimulus alpha activity, P1, and N1 components. *Neuroimage, 125*, 25–35.

Spaak, E. & de Lange, F. (2020). Hippocampal and prefrontal theta-band mechanisms underpin implicit spatial context learning. *Journal of Neuroscience, 40*(1), 191–202.

Squire, L. R. & Zola, S. M. (1996). Structure and function of declarative and nondeclarative memory systems. *Proceedings of the National Academy of Sciences, 93*(24), 13515–13522.

Staresina, B. P. & Davachi, L. (2009). Mind the gap: Binding experiences across space and time in the human hippocampus. *Neuron, 63*(2), 267–276.

Sussman, E. D., Bishop, H., Madnick, B. & Walter, R. (1985). Driver inattention and highway safety. *Transportation Research Record, 1047*, 40–48.

Taatgen, N. A., Juvina, I., Schipper, M., Borst, J. P. & Martens, S. (2009). Too much control can hurt: A threaded cognition model of the attentional blink. *Cognitive Psychology, 59*(1), 1–29.

Theeuwes, J. (1989). Effects of location and form cuing on the allocation of attention in the visual field. *Acta Psychologica, 72*(2), 177–192.

Theeuwes, J. (1990). Perceptual selectivity is task dependent: Evidence from selective search. *Acta Psychologica, 74*(1), 81–99.

Theeuwes, J. (1991a). Cross-dimensional perceptual selectivity. *Perception & Psychophysics, 50*(2), 184–193.

Theeuwes, J. (1991b). Exogenous and endogenous control of attention: The effect of visual onsets and offsets. *Attention, Perception, & Psychophysics, 49*(1), 83–90.

Theeuwes, J. (1992). Perceptual selectivity for color and form. *Perception & Psychophysics, 51*(6), 599–606.

Theeuwes, J. (1994a). Endogenous and exogenous control of visual selection. *Perception, 23*(4), 429–440.

Theeuwes, J. (1994b). Stimulus-driven capture and attentional set: Selective search for color and visual abrupt onsets. *Journal of Experimental Psychology: Human Perception and Performance, 20*(4), 799–806. http://doi.org/10.1037/0096-1523.20.4.799

Theeuwes, J. (1995). Abrupt luminance change pops out; abrupt color change does not. *Perception & Psychophysics, 57*(5), 637–644.

Theeuwes, J. (2004). Top-down search strategies cannot override attentional capture. *Psychonomic Bulletin & Review, 11*(1), 65–70.

Theeuwes, J. (2010). Top-down and bottom-up control of visual selection. *Acta Psychologica, 135*(2), 77–99.

Theeuwes, J. (2013). Feature-based attention: It is all bottom-up priming. *Philosophical Transactions of the Royal Society of London B: Biological Sciences, 368*(1628), 20130055.

Theeuwes, J. (2018). Visual selection: Usually fast and automatic; seldom slow and volitional. *Journal of Cognition, 1*(1), 1–15. http://doi.org/10.5334/joc.13

Theeuwes, J. (2019). Goal-driven, stimulus-driven and history-driven selection. *Current Opinion in Psychology, 29*, 97–101.

Theeuwes, J., Atchley, P. & Kramer, A. F. (2000). On the time course of top-down and bottom-up control of visual attention. *Control of Cognitive Processes: Attention and Performance XVIII*, 105–124.

Theeuwes, J. & Belopolsky, A. V. (2012). Reward grabs the eye: Oculomotor capture by rewarding stimuli. *Vision Research, 74*, 80–85.

Theeuwes, J. & Burger, R. (1998). Attentional control during visual search: The effect of irrelevant singletons. *Journal of Experimental Psychology: Human*

Perception and Performance, 24(5), 1342–1353. http://doi.org/10.1037 /0096-1523.24.5.1342

Theeuwes, J. & Godthelp, H. (1995). Self-explaining roads. *Safety Science*, *19*, 217–225.

Theeuwes, J., Kramer, A. F., Hahn, S. & Irwin, D. E. (1998). Our eyes do not always go where we want them to go: Capture of the eyes by new objects. *Psychological Science*, *9*(5), 379–385.

Theeuwes, J., Kramer, A. F., Hahn, S., Irwin, D. E. & Zelinsky, G. J. (1999). Influence of attentional capture on oculomotor control. *Journal of Experimental Psychology: Human Perception and Performance*, *25*(6), 1595–1608. http://doi.org/10.1037/0096-1523.25.6.1595

Theeuwes, J., Olivers, C. N. & Chizk, C. L. (2005). Remembering a location makes the eyes curve away. *Psychological Science*, *16*(3), 196–199.

Theeuwes, J., Reimann, B. & Mortier, K. (2006). Visual search for featural singletons: No top-down modulation, only bottom-up priming. *Visual Cognition*, *14*(4–8), 466–489.

Theeuwes, J. & Van der Burg, E. (2007). The role of spatial and nonspatial information in visual selection. *Journal of Experimental Psychology: Human Perception and Performance*, *33*(6), 1335–1351. http://doi.org/10.1037 /0096-1523.33.6.1335

Theeuwes, J. & Van der Burg, E. (2011). On the limits of top-down control of visual selection. *Attention, Perception, & Psychophysics*, *73*(7), 2092–2103.

Theeuwes, J. & Van der Burg, E. (2013). Priming makes a stimulus more salient. *Journal of Vision*, *13*(3), 21. http://doi.org/10.1167/13.3.21

Theeuwes, J., Van der Horst, A. R. A. & Kuiken, M (2012). *Designing safe road systems: A human factors perspective*. Burlington: Ashgate.

Thomas, N. W. & Paré, M. (2007). Temporal processing of saccade targets in parietal cortex area LIP during visual search. *Journal of Neurophysiology*, *97* (1), 942–947.

Thompson, K. G. & Bichot, N. P. (2005). A visual salience map in the primate frontal eye field. *Progress in Brain Research*, *147*, 249–262.

Thompson, K. G., Hanes, D. P., Bichot, N. P. & Schall, J. D. (1996). Perceptual and motor processing stages identified in the activity of macaque frontal eye field neurons during visual search. *Journal of Neurophysiology*, *76*, 4040–4055.

Thorndike, E. L. (1911). *Animal intelligence: Experimental studies*. New York: Macmillan.

Tipper, S. P., Howard, L. A. & Jackson, S. R. (1997). Selective reaching to grasp: Evidence for distractor interference effects. *Visual Cognition*, *4*(1), 1–38.

Todd, J. T. & Van Gelder, P. (1979). Implications of a transient-sustained dichotomy for the measurement of human performance. *Journal of Experimental Psychology: Human Perception and Performance, 5*(4), 625–638. http://doi.org/10.1037/0096-1523.5.4.625

Treisman, A. (1988). Features and objects: The fourteenth Bartlett memorial lecture. *Quarterly Journal of Experimental Psychology Section A, 40*(2), 201–237.

Tseng, Y. C. & Lleras, A. (2013). Rewarding context accelerates implicit guidance in visual search. *Attention, Perception, & Psychophysics, 75*(2), 287–298.

Tulving, E. & Schacter, D. L. (1990). Priming and human memory systems. *Science, 247*(4940), 301–306.

Turk-Browne, N. B. (2012). Statistical learning and its consequences. *Nebraska Symposium on Motivation, 59*, 117–146.

Turk-Browne, N. B., Jungé, J. A. & Scholl, B. J. (2005). The automaticity of visual statistical learning. *Journal of Experimental Psychology: General, 134*(4), 552–564. http://doi.org/10.1037/0096-3445.134.4.552

Van der Stigchel, S., Belopolsky, A. V., Peters J.C., Wijnen, J. G., Meeter, M. & Theeuwes, J. (2009a). The limits of top-down control of visual attention. *Acta Psychologica, 132*, 201–212.

Van der Stigchel, S., Mulckhuyse, M. & Theeuwes, J. (2009b). Eye cannot see it: The interference of subliminal distractors on saccade metrics. *Vision Research, 49*(16), 2104–2109.

Van der Stigchel, S. & Theeuwes, J (2006). Faces capture attention: Evidence from inhibition of return. *Visual Cognition, 13*(6), 657–665.

Van Moorselaar, D. & Slagter, H. A. (2019). Learning what is irrelevant or relevant: Expectations facilitate distractor inhibition and target facilitation through distinct neural mechanisms. *Journal of Neuroscience, 39*(35), 6953–6967.

Vecera, S. P. & Rizzo, M. (2004). What are you looking at? Impaired "social attention" following frontal-lobe damage. *Neuropsychologia, 42*, 1657–1665.

Võ, M. L. H. & Wolfe, J. M. (2013). Differential electrophysiological signatures of semantic and syntactic scene processing. *Psychological Science, 24*(9), 1816–1823.

Vuilleumier, P. (2015). Affective and motivational control of vision. *Current Opinion in Neurology, 28*(1), 29–35.

Wallenstein, G. V., Eichenbaum, H. & Hasselmo, M. E. (1998). The hippocampus as an associator of discontiguous events. *Trends in Neuroscience, 21*, 317–323.

Wang, B., Samara, I. & Theeuwes, J. (2019). Statistical regularities bias overt attention. *Attention, Perception, & Psychophysics*, 1–9.

Wang, B. & Theeuwes, J. (2018a). How to inhibit a distractor location? Statistical learning versus active, top-down suppression. *Attention, Perception, & Psychophysics*, 1–11.

Wang, B. & Theeuwes, J. (2018b). Statistical regularities modulate attentional capture. *Journal of Experimental Psychology: Human Perception and Performance*, *44*(1), 13–17. http://doi.org/10.1037/xhp0000472

Wang, B. & Theeuwes, J. (2018c). Statistical regularities modulate attentional capture independent of search strategy. *Attention, Perception, & Psychophysics*, *80*(7), 1763–1774.

Wang, B. & Theeuwes, J. (2020). Implicit attentional biases in a changing environment. *Acta Psychologia*. http://doi.org/10.1016/j.actpsy.2020.103064

Wang, B. & Theeuwes, J. (in press). Salience determines attentional orienting in visual selection. *Journal of Experimental Psychology: Human Perception and Performance*.

Wang, B., Van Driel, J., Ort, E. & Theeuwes, J. (2019). Anticipatory distractor suppression elicited by statistical regularities in visual search. *Journal of Cognitive Neuroscience*, 1–14.

White, B. J., Berg, D. J., Kan, J. Y., Marino, R. A., Itti, L. & Munoz, D. P. (2017). Superior colliculus neurons encode a visual saliency map during free viewing of natural dynamic video. *Nature Communications*, *8*, 14263.

Wolfe, J. (2018). Everything is foreseen, yet free will is given (Mishna Avot 3: 15). *Journal of Cognition*, *1*(1).

Wolfe, J. M., Butcher, S. J., Lee, C. & Hyle, M. (2003). Changing your mind: On the contributions of top-down and bottom-up guidance in visual search for feature singletons. *Journal of Experimental Psychology: Human Perception and Performance*, *29*(2), 483.

Won, B. Y., Kosoyan, M. & Geng, J. J. (2019). Evidence for second-order singleton suppression based on probabilistic expectations. *Journal of Experimental Psychology: Human Perception and Performance*, *45*(1), 125–128. http://doi.org/10.1037/xhp0000594

Won, B. Y. & Leber, A. B. (2016). How do magnitude and frequency of monetary reward guide visual search? *Attention, Perception, & Psychophysics*, 1–11.

Wyble, B., Bowman, H. & Nieuwenstein, M. (2009). The attentional blink provides episodic distinctiveness: Sparing at a cost. *Journal of Experimental Psychology: Human Perception and Performance*, *35*(3), 787–807. http://doi.org/10.1037/a0013902

Yamamoto, S., Monosov, I. E., Yasuda, M. & Hikosaka, O. (2012). What and where information in the caudate tail guides saccades to visual objects. *Journal of Neuroscience, 32*(32), 11005–11016.

Yantis, S. & Egeth, H. E. (1999). On the distinction between visual salience and stimulus-driven attentional capture. *Journal of Experimental Psychology: Human Perception and Performance, 25*(3), 661–676. http://doi.org/10 .1037/0096-1523.25.3.661

Yantis, S. & Hillstrom, A. P. (1994). Stimulus-driven attentional capture: Evidence from equiluminant visual objects. *Journal of Experimental Psychology: Human Perception and Performance, 20*(1), 95–107. http://doi .org/10.1037/0096-1523.20.1.95

Yantis, S. & Jonides, J. (1984). Abrupt visual onsets and selective attention: Evidence from visual search. *Journal of Experimental Psychology: Human Perception and Performance, 10*(5), 601–621. http://doi.org/10.1037/0096-1523.10.5.601

Yasuda, M. & Hikosaka, O. (2015). Functional territories in primate substantia nigra pars reticulata separately signaling stable and flexible values. *Journal of Neurophysiology, 113*(6), 1681–1696.

Yeterian, E. H. & Van Hoesen, G. W. (1978). Cortico-striate projections in the rhesus monkey: The organization of certain cortico-caudate connections. *Brain Research, 139*(1), 43–63.

Zelinsky, G. J. & Bisley, J. W. (2015). The what, where, and why of priority maps and their interactions with visual working memory. *Annals of the New York Academy of Sciences, 1339*(1), 154–164.

Zhang, X., Zhaoping, L., Zhou, T. & Fang, F. (2012). Neural activities in V1 create a bottom-up saliency map. *Neuron, 73*(1), 183–192.

Zhao, J., Al-Aidroos, N. & Turk-Browne, N. B. (2013). Attention is spontaneously biased toward regularities. *Psychological Science, 24*(5), 667–677.

Zhaoping, L. (2008). Attention capture by eye of origin singletons even without awareness: A hallmark of a bottom-up saliency map in the primary visual cortex. *Journal of Vision, 8*(5), 1.1–18.

Acknowledgments

Jan Theeuwes was supported by a European Research Council (ERC) advanced grant 833029 – [LEARNATTEND].

Michel Failing was supported by funding of the Alexander von Humboldt foundation.

Cambridge Elements ☰

Perception

James T. Enns
The University of British Columbia

Editor James T. Enns is Professor at the University of British Columbia, where he researches the interaction of perception, attention, emotion, and social factors. He has previously been Editor of the *Journal of Experimental Psychology: Human Perception and Performance* and Associate Editor at *Psychological Science, Consciousness and Cognition, Attention Perception & Psychophysics,* and *Visual Cognition.*

About the Series
The modern study of human perception includes event perception, bidirectional influences between perception and action, music, language, the integration of the senses, human action observation, and the important roles of emotion, motivation, and social factors. Each Element in the series combines authoritative literature reviews of foundational topics with forward-looking presentations of the recent developments on a given topic.

Cambridge Elements ≡

Perception

Printed in the United States
By Bookmasters